Freezer to Oven to Table

FREEZER
TO
OVEN
TO
TABLE

CEIL DYER

ARBOR HOUSE
NEW YORK

Published in the United States by
Arbor House Publishing Company, Inc., New York,
and simultaneously in Canada by
Clarke, Irwin & Company Ltd.

Library of Congress Catalogue Card Number: 75–31075

ISBN: 0–87795–128–4 cloth; 0–87795–134–9 paper

Manufactured in the United States of America

Contents

Freezer to Oven to Table

Introduction

FROM FREEZER TO OVEN TO TABLE
WITH SNEAKY FREEZER COOKERY

Preparing a dozen or so casserole dishes now to bake later is a great idea, but you'll need a lot of freezer space to hold them, especially if you intend freezing all of them in serving casseroles. You'll need a dozen or so casseroles, too. But it can be done, and you'll have just that many easy-to-get-to-the-table meals stashed away for whenever you need a vacation from heavy cooking.

Cooking for the freezer in this way is great. However, it takes time and plenty of it. What I call sneaky freezer cooking is ever so much easier, faster and more fun.

Sneaky freezer cooking for and from the freezer is what this book is about. It's not a "make work" but a "save you time, work and money" cookbook.

If you are like me, you enjoy serving your family and friends really great meals. It's pleasurable to bask in the sunshine of their admiration, and cooking can be enjoyable—sometimes. But not every day, day in and day out. That's a bore. I cook only when I'm in the mood because by sneaky freezer cookery-

—making enough of a basic recipe to provide the fundamentals for two totally different dishes—I need only do heavy cooking once for two meals. Obviously, there's less work and fewer dishes to wash. The budget benefits, too. Casserole dishes that are ideal for freezing are almost always economical fare.

Unlike other freezer methods that often give the poor cook only the thin end of the wedge—much work with little result—sneaky freezing makes for both an easy-cooking and a great-tasting life.

If you don't have enough dishes that can go from freezer to oven to keep your stockpile of frozen foods, line them with heavy-duty foil. Spoon in the ingredients to be frozen, wrap well and freeze. When the dish is frozen solid, remove the foil packet, return the dish to your kitchen cupboard and it's again ready for use. When you are ready to cook the meal, unwrap and return the frozen food to its original casserole for quick reheating or baking.

Label and date all dishes that go in your freezer. If properly wrapped, they will keep at zero temperature for five or six months. If the temperature is above zero, however, serve them much sooner, within a week or two.

A Few Words about Freezing Sneaky Style

Just slightly undercook portion to be frozen. Meat should be tender but still a bit firm. Ladle hot foods into freezer-to-oven-to-table baking dishes, foil pans or unbreakable casseroles. Cool quickly by placing container in ice water. Wrap and freeze immediately. Freezer wrapping must be moisture proof and vapor proof—in other words, air tight. Cover and seal top of dish with foil, then double wrap in foil or place in substantial plastic freezer bag that can be completely sealed.

Store in frozen food compartment of your refrigerator no

longer than three to four weeks. It operates at 15° to 20° and is only suitable for short-term storage. You may safely store in a home freezer operating at zero temperature for longer periods, in most cases up to three months, but for best flavor it's wise to use precooked and seasoned dishes within the month.

What Freezer?

A freezing unit with a separate door that is part of the refrigerator is the least expensive way to acquire a freezer. However, it will cost you the most to operate and it is not recommended for long-term freezing since the temperature control is not consistent as in a free-standing freezer.

Free-standing freezers are available in either upright or chest models. The chest model is the less expensive of the two. However, this model necessitates a lot of bending and searching for the particular item you want, inevitably at the very bottom, and your hands do get cold. If it's any compensation, however, when closed the flat top can be used as a work surface. Upright models cost more both to buy and to operate. The costs are justified perhaps by these decided advantages: upright freezers take up less space in the kitchen, searching for packages is much less of a problem, and uprights are easier to defrost. Uprights also come with automatic defrosters, but again the cost goes up, and there is some loss of freezing space.

What Won't Freeze?

It would be easier, far easier, to list those foods that will not freeze successfully than to list those that will. Put these few on your "Do Not Freeze" list and consider everything else freezable

Gelatin salds and desserts: They become rubbery and "weepy."

Mayonnaise: It curdles unless used in very small proportions with other ingredients.

Stuffing (in raw or prepared and cooked poultry): The stuffing will be lukewarm long after the outside of the bird is overcooked.

Hard-cooked egg whites: They become rubbery unless finely chopped and used in a small ratio to other ingredients.

Raw salad ingredients: Crispness is lost (exception: green pepper).

Sour Cream: It separates.

Boiled Frosting: It becomes sticky.

Boiled white potatoes: Unless in sauce, they become mealy.

Finally, and most important, do not refreeze completely thawed cooked frozen food. This does not apply to blanched or raw frozen vegetables, frozen fruit, frozen boiled or raw shellfish, or raw frozen meat when these are to be used as an ingredient and then refrozen.

How to Wrap

There are so many wonderful freezer materials on the market that it would be impossible to give more than a general list. However, to my way of thinking, the best investments are ovenproof dishes and casseroles that go from freezer to oven to table. To wrap them you can use heavy-duty aluminum foil and plastic wrap, handy reusable polyethylene bags, or those quick-and-easy plastic bags that snap from a roll. For secure sealing there is freezer tape, cellophane tape, plastic-coated wire ties and plain fashioned rubber bands. Most important—whatever you use—wrap securely, and make sure your package is moisture proof, vapor proof, and strong enough to hold the particular food you plan to store.

There is no need to thaw the main course dishes in this book before reheating. They can go directly from freezer to oven to table. Time to reheat depends on the quantity and type of food, but the shallower the baking dish, the more quickly to the table. The rule of thumb—at 425° allow 40 to 60 minutes.

1

From the Stew Pot

Real old-fashioned stews take time to prepare but there's nothing difficult about them. You can prepare the basic recipe, add stew vegetables to one part, and serve. Freeze the remainder in one-pint containers and you have the basis for a number of interesting and different quick-to-the-table dishes. Or pour all into freezer-to-oven-to-table casseroles, wrap and freeze. In each serving variation given here, additional vegetables or seasonings are added in the last few minutes of cooking for peak flavor and texture.

BEEF STEW BASE

3½ pounds lean, boneless beef, cut into 1-inch cubes
½ pound beef marrow bones or knuckle bones
1 cup red wine
   Water
2 large carrots, scraped and cut into several pieces
1 large onion, peeled and quartered
½ cup mushroom stems (optional)
   Several sprigs parsley
   Salt
   Freshly ground black pepper

Place meat cubes and bones in bottom of a large roasting pan in preheated 450° oven. Bake until cubes and bones are browned, turning them several times to brown on all sides. Remove from oven and transfer to a large (6-quart) stock pot. Add the wine and sufficient water (about 4 quarts) to cover meat and bones by at least 4 inches. Bring to a full boil, lower heat. Add remaining ingredients and let simmer 2½ to 3 hours or until meat is sufficiently tender to pierce easily with the tip of a small sharp knife. Remove and discard bones. Use a slotted spoon to remove meat and vegetables (discard vegetables). Put ⅓ of meat (to serve without freezing) into a large bowl. Put remaining meat, dividing equally, into 1-pint containers. Cover bowl of meat with stock (using about ⅓). Cover meat in containers with remaining stock, filling them about ¾ full to allow for expansion when frozen. If there is any remaining stock, pour it into another container and use it for any recipe using basic stock as an ingredient. Refrigerate bowl of meat and filled freezer containers until all fat has come to the surface. Remove and discard fat. Cover containers, wrap and freeze until ready to use. Makes about 6 pints stew base.

CLASSIC FRENCH BEEF STEW

4 cups stew base
8 to 12 baby carrots, scrapes, or 4 to 6 medium-sized
carrots cut into thick chunky slices
8 to 10 small white onions peeled

Reheat stew base to boiling. Lower heat to simmer. Add vegetables and let simmer until tender. Correct seasoning with salt and pepper. Serve at once or pour into freezer-to-oven-to-table casserole, wrap and freeze. To serve place in preheated 350° oven until bubbly hot.

Serves 4 to 6.

HAWAIIAN BEEF STEW

2 1-pint containers frozen beef stew base
½ cup beef stock or water
2 tablespoons tomato catsup
2 10-ounce packages frozen Hawaiian-style vegetables with
pineapple and seasoning sauce
Cooked white rice

Place containers of frozen stew in a pan of warm water until sufficiently thawed to transfer to an oven-to-table casserole. Add stock or water, cover and bake at 350° until meat cubes are sufficiently thawed to separate. Stir in tomato catsup, increase heat to 400° and continue baking until meat is thoroughly heated. Add vegetables, fork-stir until blended. Cover and bake for a final 10 to 15 minutes. Serve over hot rice.

Serves 4 to 6.

ITALIAN BEEF STEW

2 1-pint containers frozen beef stew base
½ cup beef stock or water
1 tablespoon tomato paste
2 10-ounce packages frozen Italian-style vegetables
   with seasoned sauce
1 1-pound package flat noodles, cooked according to package
   directions

Place containers of frozen stew in a pan of warm water until sufficiently thawed to transfer to an oven-to-table casserole. Add stock or water, cover and bake at 350° until meat cubes can be separated. Stir in tomato paste, cover and continue to bake at 400° until meat is thoroughly hot. Add frozen vegetables and fork-stir until blended. Cover and bake a final 10 to 15 minutes, or until vegetables are hot. Serve over hot noodles.

Serves 4 to 6.

TEXAN BEEF STEW

2 1-pint containers frozen beef stew base
½ cup beef stock or water
1 8-ounce can tomato sauce
1 tablespoon cider vinegar
1 tablespoon brown sugar
1 tablespoon Worcestershire sauce
1 tablespoon chili powder
1 1-pound can kidney beans, drained

Place containers of frozen stew in pan of warm water until sufficiently thawed to transfer to a large oven-to-table casserole. Add stock or water, cover and bake at 350° until meat cubes can be separated with a fork. Add remaining ingredients, fork-stir to blend, adjust oven heat to 400° and continue to bake until thoroughly heated—about one hour.

Serves 4 to 6.

BAVARIAN BEEF STEW

  2 1-pint containers frozen beef stew base
  ½ cup dry red wine
  ½ cup beef stock or water
  6 ginger snaps crushed into fine crumbs
  2 teaspoons sugar
  1 tablespoon red wine vinegar
  1 small crisp fresh green cabbage, trimmed, cored and cut
     into wedges
     Steamed new potatoes

Place containers of beef stew in pan of warm water until sufficiently thawed to transfer to an oven-to-table casserole. Add wine. Add ginger snap crumbs to stock or water, cover and set aside. Bake meat at 350° until cubes can be separated. Stir in remaining stock—crumb mixture, sugar and vinegar. Continue to bake, covered, until thoroughly heated. Place cabbage wedges on top of meat, cover and let bake for final 25 to 30 minutes, until cabbage is tender. Serve with potatoes.

Serves 4 to 6

I like soul-satisfying fare and there's nothing like this homemade beef stew to satisfy anyone's soul. At the same time that you prepare it, a Middle East stew with lentils goes into the freezer ready for the night when you don't feel like cooking anything. Add fresh fruit and cheese for dessert, and dinner is served.

BEEF STEW with DUMPLINGS
and
MIDDLE EAST BEEF and LENTIL STEW

Essentially, these recipes are for one basic stew to which different ingredients are added for two totally different-tasting dishes. Though the stew with dumplings is suggested for "now," it may be poured into a freezer-to-oven-to-table casserole, wrapped and frozen, and served with crusty French bread instead of dumplings when reheated.

Stew Base

3 pounds boneless chuck or round
½ cup flour
2 teaspoons salt
¼ teaspoon pepper
¼ cup rendered bacon or salt port fat
6 cups water
1 onion, chopped
1 bay leaf
1½ teaspoons dried thyme leaves

Cut meat into even 1½-inch cubes. On waxed paper mix flour with salt and pepper. Roll beef cubes in mixture, coating evenly on all sides. Reserve remaining flour mixture. Heat the rendered fat in a large heavy pot. In it brown beef cubes a few at a time. Do not overcrowd the pan. As beef cubes are browned, remove and set aside. When all are browned, pour off and discard any remaining fat from the pot, wipe pot clean with paper toweling and return meat to it. Add water, onion, bay leaf and thyme. Bring to a boil; reduce heat and simmer, partially covered, for 1 hour.

For Middle East Beef and Lentil Stew

1½ cups lentils
¼ teaspoon oregano

Transfer half of the meat to a freezer casserole dish. Cover with the lentils. Sprinkle with the oregano and pour about 2½ cups of the hot stock over all. Place in a preheated oven and bake for about 45 minutes. Cool slightly, cover, wrap and freeze.

Serves 6 to 8.

For Beef Stew with Dumplings

8 small white onions, peeled
6 small carrots, scraped and halved crosswise
8 small white new potatoes with skins on, scraped and scrubbed
4 small turnips, peeled and halved

Let remaining stew in pot continue to simmer for another hour. Add onions, carrots, and potatoes. Let simmer 30 minutes. Add turnips and continue to cook until vegetables are almost tender. If stew is to be frozen, pour into freezer-to-oven-to-table casserole. Wrap to freeze, or, to serve without freezing, prepare dumplings as below and continue as directed.

For Dumplings

2 cups packaged biscuit mix
1 egg
½ cup milk
3 tablespoons flour
¼ cup cold water

Put biscuit mix in a mixing bowl, stir in egg and milk, mixing with a fork until just blended. Drop batter by rounded table-spoons onto simmering stew, directly over vegetables and meat (not in liquid—this makes them soggy), 2 to 3 inches apart, to allow for expansion. Cook uncovered over low heat for 10 minutes, cover and cook 10 minutes longer. Remove dumplings with a slotted spoon to a heated dish. Stir the flour into the cold water and stir into stew. Cook, stirring until liquid thickens. Replace dumplings on top of stew. Reheat, covered, until thoroughly hot. Serve from the pot.

Serves 6 to 8.

To serve frozen stew: Remove freezer wrap. Cover and bake for 30 minutes in a preheated 400° oven, uncover and fork-stir. Continue to bake until thoroughly heated.

Here is an easy beef stew with a wonderful Italian flavor, equally good with noodles or rice, so have half tonight with peppers over pasta and freeze the rest with onions for serving with rice, North Italian-style (or vice versa, of course). Serve plenty of Parmesan cheese with both.

ITALIAN STEW with GREEN PEPPERS
and
ITALIAN STEW with LITTLE WHITE ONIONS

Stew Base

3 pounds beef stew meat
½ cup flour mixed with 2 teaspoons seasoned salt
3 tablespoons vegetable oil
1 large Italian purple onion, chopped
1 clove garlic, minced
½ teaspoon mixed Italian herbs
1 1-pound can Italian tomatoes with basil
1 tablespoon red wine vinegar
2 cups water

For Stew with Onions

8 to 12 very small white onions
1 1-pound package flat noodles, cooked according
   to package directions
   Salt

For Stew with Green Peppers

3 medium-sized green peppers, seeded and cut into
   1½-inch pieces
   Cooked rice

Cut meat into 1-inch cubes. Roll in seasoned flour. Shake off excess flour and reserve. Heat 1 tablespoon of the oil in a large heavy pot over medium-high heat. Add a few of the beef cubes and brown quickly on all sides. As each cube is browned, remove it and replace it with a fresh cube. Add additional oil to the pot as needed. When all meat cubes are browned remove them from the pot and drain all but a thin film of oil from the pot. Add the chopped onion and garlic, stir-fry for about 1 minute. Add all of the browned meat. Sprinkle with reserved flour, fork-stir, then add remaining ingredients except onions and green peppers. Partially cover the pot and let simmer for about 1½ hours, or until meat is sufficiently tender to pierce easily with a small sharp knife. Remove from heat. Ladle portion to be frozen into a freezer-to-oven-to-table casserole and add the onions. Cover and bake in a 375° oven for about 30 minutes. Cool slightly. Cover, wrap and freeze.

Ladle portion to be served into a second ovenproof casserole and add green peppers. Cover and bake until meat is tender. Serve over freshly cooked noodles.

To serve frozen casserole: Remove freezer wrap, cover and bake for 1 hour in preheated 400° oven. Uncover, fork-stir, and continue to bake until bubbly hot. Serve over hot rice.

Makes 8 total servings.

2

International Classics

From my international file, a collection of favorites.

Double up recipes from many countries, each enough for "tonight" and a casserole for the freezer, or freeze both for spectacular buffet suppers, or two dinners, that are ready when you are.

VERSATILE CARBONNADE FLAMANDE
(Beef Stew with Beer)

This recipe makes a total of 12 servings. It can be frozen for easy reheating and serving in two freezer-to-oven-to-table casserole dishes—each to serve 6. Or you can serve part without freezing and freeze the remainder for a second meal. Just before serving you can add to either portion small boiled white onions (2 for each serving) and/or scraped boiled baby carrots (3 for each serving) and/or sautéed fresh mushroom caps (3 per serving) or sautéed green pepper strips (3 per serving).

This stew can be served with crusty French bread or boiled new potatoes, or over pasta or rice.

4 pounds chuck steak cut in 2-inch cubes
5 tablespoons butter
2 cloves garlic, minced
1 cup chopped mild onion
2 cups beer
2 cups beef stock
2 tablespoons flour
½ teaspoon salt
¼ teaspoon coarsely ground black pepper

Put meat in bottom of broiler pan, place in preheated 400° oven until each cube is browned, turning cubes several times so they are evenly browned on all sides. Heat 3 tablespoons of the butter in a large deep skillet or stew pot. Add garlic and onions and sauté until limp. Add browned meat cubes, beer and stock. Season with salt and pepper. Cover, turn heat to low and let simmer for about 1½ hours, or until meat is tender. In a small skillet melt remaining 2 tablespoons butter, stir in flour and cook over very low heat, stirring very often for 10 to 15 minutes, until mixture is deep golden in color and gives off a fragrant nutlike aroma. Stir this into the stew and continue to cook until gravy is thick and smooth. Taste for seasoning and add additional salt and pepper if desired. If desired serve part "now," ladle remainder into a freezer-to-oven-to-table baking dish, wrap and freeze for a second meal.

To serve frozen portion: Unwrap and bake covered in a preheated 400° oven for 1 hour, or until bubbly hot.

VIENNESE GOULASH
and
VEAL with CAPERS and SOUR CREAM

Basic Recipe

2 tablespoons paprika
½ cup flour
3 pounds lean veal, cut into 1½-inch cubes
2 tablespoons salad oil
1 tablespoon butter
1 large onion, chopped
1 large fresh tomato, chopped
1 1-pound can stewed tomatoes
2 cups water
1 cup dry white wine
1 6-ounce can tomato paste
  Salt
  Pepper
  Water (optional)

For the Goulash

1 1-pound package of flat noodles, cooked according to
  package directions
½ cup minced parsley

For the Veal with Capers and Sour Cream

2 tablespoons capers, drained
1 cup sour cream
8 to 12 steamed new potatoes

Mix paprika and flour and rub into each cube of meat. Heat
the oil in a deep heavy pot. In it brown the meat cubes a few at a
time. Remove each cube as browned and replace it with
another one. Add additional oil if needed. When all cubes are
browned pour off and discard the cooking oil and add the butter
to the pot. Add the onion and sauté until limp. Return the
browned meat to the pot and add the fresh tomato, canned
tomatoes, water and wine. Stir in tomato paste and season
lightly with salt and pepper. Bring to a boil, then lower heat
and let simmer for about 1 hour or until meat is sufficiently
tender to pierce easily with a small kitchen knife.

Remove half of meat and place in a freezer-to-oven-to-table
baking dish. Spoon half of the sauce over the surface. Wrap and
freeze.

If remaining stew is to be served without freezing, let it
simmer in the remaining sauce until very tender—about 30
minutes. Or pour into a second casserole, wrap and freeze.
When ready to serve reheat 1 hour in 400° oven. In either case,
when stew is hot spoon over just-cooked noodles. Sprinkle with
parsley and serve at once.

Serves 4 to 6.

To serve veal with capers and sour cream: Unwrap frozen casserole and bake covered in preheated 400° oven for 1 hour. Uncover, stir in capers and sour cream. Bake uncovered until thoroughly heated. Serve with steamed new potatoes.

Serves 4 to 6.

POT AU FEU

Pot au feu is more than one meal—it's two or three and more. You can serve either the meat or chicken part "now" or freeze either or both for later. You can "eat now" or "freeze for later" the broth and vegetables for a superb meatless main course soup; and you can use any leftover broth—either fresh or frozen—as the base for gravy or sauce for yet another meal.

3 pounds brisket of beef
1 shinbone of beef or 1 veal knuckle
2 quarts water
1 teaspoon salt
2 medium-sized onions, peeled and quartered
6 or 8 medium-sized carrots, scraped and cut into large
    chunks
2 cloves garlic, peeled
4 small white turnips, peeled and cut in half
2½ to 3 pounds chicken legs and thighs

Optional additions:
¼ to ½ cup trimmed and chopped mushroom stems
2 to 3 tablespoons minced parsley stems
2 to 3 chopped leafy celery tops

Place beef and shinbone or veal knuckle in a large stew pot. In a second pot bring the water to a full boil, then pour it over meat and bone. Bring water again to a full boil and skim surface until clear. Add salt, one of the onions, one of the carrots and the garlic. Lower heat, partially cover the pot and let simmer for 2 hours. Add remaining vegetables and chicken, and any or all of the optional additions. Partially cover and let simmer until meat and chicken and all vegetables are tender. Cool slightly. Then remove meat, chicken and vegetables to a deep casserole dish and pour about ½ cup of the broth over them. Cover and refrigerate.

Strain remaining stock into a large bowl, cover and refrigerate until all fat has risen to the surface and congealed. Remove and discard fat. Transfer broth to a large pot and add meat, chicken and vegetables. Reheat to steaming hot. Serve part now. Ladle remaining meat and/or chicken and vegetables into a freezer-to-oven-to-table casserole and cover with broth. Wrap and freeze. Pour any remaining broth into a freezer jar, filling it no more than ¾ full to allow for expansion when frozen. Wrap and freeze.

To serve frozen casserole: Unwrap and place in a 400° preheated oven. Bake covered 1 hour, uncover, fork-stir and continue to bake until steamy hot.

To reheat broth: Unwrap container and place in a pan of cold water until sufficiently thawed to slide into a small saucepan. Add about 2 tablespoons water and place over low heat until thawed and heated.

LAMB NAVARIN

¾ cup flour
1 teaspoon salt
½ teaspoon pepper
3 pounds lean lamb, cut into 2-inch cubes
   Oil for browning meat

 1 tablespoon butter
 1 clove garlic, minced
 1 cup chicken stock (see p. 143)
 1 cup dry white wine
 1 cup orange juice
 ¼ cup white wine vinegar
 1 tablespoon sugar
 6 medium-sized carrots, scraped and cut into 2-inch pieces
12 very small white onions
   Salt
   Pepper
 1 10-ounce package frozen green beans (for one portion)
 1 10-ounce package frozen peas (for second portion)

Combine flour, salt and pepper on waxed paper. Roll lamb cubes in mixture until coated; shake off excess flour. Cover the bottom of a large heavy pot with a thin layer of oil. Heat to almost smoking, add a few of the lamb cubes and brown quickly on all sides. Remove each cube as browned and replace with another cube. Keep adding oil as needed until all meat is browned. Pour any remaining cooking oil from pot and add butter. When melted add garlic and sauté until soft. Return meat to skillet. Pour in stock, wine, orange juice and vinegar. Bring to a boil, then lower heat, stir in sugar and let simmer until lamb is sufficiently tender to pierce easily with a small kitchen knife. Add carrots and onions and continue to simmer until vegetables are almost tender. Ladle portion to be frozen into a freezer-to-oven-to-table baking dish. Wrap and freeze.

Correct seasoning of portion to be served without freezing, adding salt and pepper as needed. Add frozen beans. Cover and cook until all vegetables are tender. Serve with crusty French bread. (Or, if desired, may be poured into freezer-to-oven-to-table casserole, wrapped and frozen. To serve, unwrap and place in preheated 400° oven for 1 hour or until very hot.)

To serve remaining frozen portion: Unwrap and bake covered in preheated 400° oven for 1 hour. Uncover, fork-stir. Correct seasoning with salt and pepper. Add frozen peas and gently break up frozen block with a fork. Cover and continue to bake until peas are tender and stew is thoroughly heated.

Each portion serves 4 to 6.

BOEUF à la Mode (to serve now)
and
BOEUF MIROTON (for the freezer)

Prepare both dishes in the same amount of time as it takes to make just one dish.

¼ pound salt pork
5 pounds bottom or top round of beef
4 tablespoons butter
2 cups chopped onion
1 clove garlic, minced
½ cup chopped mushroom stems
3 cups beef stock or 2 cups canned beef broth,
   and 1 cup water
½ cup Madeira
2 tablespoons arrowroot (optional)
1 8-ounce can tomato sauce
2 teaspoons tomato paste
   Salt
   Freshly ground black pepper
½ cup seasoned croutons

Have the butcher wrap the meat in a thin layer of fat and tie it securely in four or five places so it will hold its shape while cooking.

Wash the salt pork until it is free of loose salt. Blot dry and cut it into small cubes. Place them in a large heavy pot over moderate heat and cook, stirring, until all fat has been rendered and cubes are crisp. Remove cubes with a slotted spoon and set aside. Heat the rendered fat to almost smoking. Add the beef and brown it on all sides. With the aid of a spatula and heavy spoon, remove the meat and set aside. Pour off and discard fat from pot. Add butter and melt over low heat. Add onions, garlic and sauté, stirring often, until limp. Remove 1 cup of onions and set aside for freezer dish.

Add mushroom stems to pot and place meat over vegetables. Pour in stock (or broth and water) and Madeira. Bring to a full boil and let simmer until meat is tender. Remove meat and set aside at room temperature for 30 minutes. Strain cooking liquid into a bowl, pressing down on vegetables with a wooden spoon to extract all liquid. Refrigerate stock for about 30 minutes, then carefully skim off and discard surface fat. Remove 1 cup stock and set aside for freezer dish. Slice and set aside 6 or 8 thin slices of meat for freezer dish.

Return remainder of meat to cooking pot, add strained stock. (If desired, let stand at room temperature up to 2 hours, then reheat and serve, or refrigerate until time to reheat and serve.) Reheat and, if desired, to thicken stock, stir a little of the hot sauce into the arrowroot and stir this into the sauce. Serve immediately.

To prepare boeuf miroton for the freezer: Spoon half of the sautéed onion into the bottom of a long shallow freezer-to-oven-to-table baking dish and cover with the beef slices. Top with remaining onions, combine the tomato sauce, reserved stock and tomato paste in a saucepan and stir over medium heat until smooth. Taste and season lightly with salt and pepper. Place croutons between waxed paper and crush with a rolling pin, or whirl briefly in a blender to make large crumbs. Sprinkle over surface of sauce. Cover, wrap dish completely in foil and freeze. To serve: Unwrap but leave covered. Place in cold oven. Set temperature at 375° and bake 30 minutes. Uncover and continue to bake until bubbly hot.

Serves 8.

BEEFSTEAK and KIDNEY PIE with MUSHROOMS

One dish for now, one for the freezer—or freeze the whole for a party meal.

You can find this very British dish at Simpson's-in-the-Strand in London or at the sixteenth-century English pub The Cheshire Cheese, just off Fleet Street, although there they will often substitute small pieces of game for the mushrooms. Either way, it's "uncommonly good," say my British friends. I agree, and so will you if you make it up one morning and then "find" it in your freezer ready to reheat one cold and foggy night.

Filling

      3 pounds round steak
      6 heaping tablespoons flour
      6 tablespoons butter
    1½ pounds veal kidneys
      ½ cup chopped onions
      ½ pound sliced mushrooms
      2 tablespoons flour
      2 cups dry red wine
      1 cup beef stock
      1 bay leaf
      ¼ teaspoon mace
      ¼ cup chopped parsley
      1 teaspoon Worcestershire sauce
      1 teaspoon salt
      ½ teaspoon pepper

Cut beef into 1-inch cubes and dredge in flour. Heat half the butter in a deep saucepan or heavy skillet, add the meat, brown it on all sides, and transfer equal amounts to two ovenproof casseroles. Remove membrane, fat and whole center core from kidneys; slice and add to pan with second half of butter; sauté for about 5 minutes and add evenly to casseroles. Sauté onions and mushrooms in skillet, stirring frequently, until onions are transparent, add flour, stir until blended, cook for one minute. Add wine, beef stock, bay leaf, mace, parsley, Worcestershire sauce, salt and pepper. Cook until thoroughly hot. Pour evenly over meat in casseroles. Cover with crust (see below), place freezer casserole in freezer until crust is firm. Wrap and freeze.

Bake casserole for now in preheated 400° oven for 10 minutes, lower heat to 300° and bake for 1 hour.

Each casserole serves 6.

Crust

2 cups flour
⅛ teaspoon salt
⅓ cup butter
⅓ cup lard
    Cold water
1 egg

Sift flour and salt into mixing bowl and cut in butter and lard. Add enough cold water to form a stiff dough (about ½ to ¾ cup) and chill for 30 minutes. Roll out half at a time on lightly floured board in two rounds about ½ inch wider than the casseroles. Beat egg lightly with a little water. Moisten rim of casseroles with beaten egg. Add crust, brush with remaining egg and water.

To serve frozen casserole: Unwrap, bake in 400° oven for 10

minutes, cut vents in pie crust and continue to bake at 350° for 1 hour.

Brussels sprouts are the traditional accompaniment to this dish, but my personal preference is a fresh spinach salad with chopped chives and crisp crumbled bacon. You'll have the bacon handy if you remember to save it in the freezer in a small jar. (Crisp it in the oven for a moment before serving.)

CHICKEN MARENGO
(A double recipe to make ahead for a party)

6 large chicken breasts, skinned and boned
3 tablespoons butter
¼ cup cognac or brandy
4 cups chicken stock
½ cup dry white wine or vermouth
1 6-ounce can tomato paste
1 4-ounce can sliced mushrooms
2 packages frozen lobster tails (two tails to a package)
2 ripe but firm tomatoes, cut into wedges
   Cooked flat noodles

Cut chicken breasts into large cubes. Heat butter in a large skillet. Add chicken cubes and sauté until meat is firm and white. Heat brandy in a small saucepan, ignite and pour flaming over chicken. Add chicken stock, stir to blend and let simmer over low heat. Combine wine and tomato paste and stir until smooth. Stir mixture into simmering chicken stock. Add sliced mushrooms and their liquid and cook over low heat for about 15 minutes. Remove from heat and ladle into a long, shallow freezer-to-oven dish. Wrap and freeze.

To serve: Preheat oven to 400°. Unwrap, cover and bake

until bubbly hot. While chicken bakes, cook lobster according to package directions. Remove meat from shell and cut into bite-sized pieces. Add lobster and tomato wedges to chicken mixture during last 10 minutes of baking. Serve over noodles. Serves 10 to 12.

BASQUE-STYLE BAKED BEANS

3 cups (1½ pounds) dried marrow or navy beans
2 tablespoons olive oil
1 clove garlic, minced
1 teaspoon Spice Parisienne, or ¼ teaspoon each of basil, marjoram, rosemary and thyme
1 1-pound can stewed tomatoes
1 large fresh tomato
1 tablespoon sugar
½ teaspoon salt
⅓ teaspoon coarsely ground black pepper
½ to 1 cup lean chopped leftover baked or boiled ham
2 tablespoons red wine vinegar
2 tablespoons finely minced parsley

Place beans in a colander and wash under cold running water. Drain and put in a 5- or 6-quart heavy pot. Add sufficient water to cover by about 2 inches. Bring to a full boil. Remove from heat and let the beans soak uncovered for one hour. Again bring the water to a full boil, lower heat, partially cover pot and let the beans simmer for about 1½ hours, or until they are tender but not mushy. (The beans should be completely covered during cooking time. If necessary, add more water as needed.) Cool slightly, then drain the beans and set them aside.

Heat the olive oil in the same cooking pot. Add the garlic and sauté until limp. Add the Spice Parisienne and stir for about 15 seconds. Add the canned and fresh tomatoes and the beans. Season with the sugar, salt and pepper, add the ham and mix together gently but thoroughly.

Ladle the portion to be frozen into a freezer-to-oven-to-table baking dish. Wrap and freeze.

Let portion to be served now simmer gently for 10 to 15 minutes. Stir in 1 tablespoon red wine vinegar, 1 tablespoon minced parsley, and serve very hot with crusty French bread to mop up the sauce.

To serve frozen portion: Unwrap and bake covered in a preheated 400° oven for 1 hour. Uncover, add 1 tablespoon vinegar, 1 tablespoon minced parsley and gently fork-stir to blend. Continue to bake until thoroughly heated. If desired, serve over just-cooked fluffy white rice. Or cook the beans without the ham and serve with kielbasa (Polish garlic sausage) or knockwurst.

INDONESIAN MEAT TURNOVERS

Pastry

4 tablespoons butter–cold
4 tablespoons vegetable shortening–cold
2 cups all-purpose flour, sifted
½ teaspoon salt
　Ice water

Cut butter and shortening into flour and salt until mixture resembles coarse ground cornmeal. Add sufficient ice water to hold dough together. With fingertips form into a ball. Cover and refrigerate 4 hours or longer. Pastry can be made a day ahead.

Filling

3 tablespoons butter
1 teaspoon curry powder
¼ pound fresh mushrooms, trimmed and finely chopped
1 small white onion, finely chopped
4 tablespoons Madeira or sherry
1½ cups finely chopped cooked pork (leftover roast pork is fine, or substitute leftover roast beef)
2 to 3 tablespoons heavy cream

Melt butter in a saucepan and stir in curry powder. Add mushrooms, onion and Madeira. Stir until liquid is smooth. Let simmer until vegetables are tender. Stir in meat, then add just enough cream to moisten mixture and hold it together. Remove from heat and cool before using.

Mushroom Sauce

3 tablespoons butter
¼ pound chopped fresh mushrooms
2 tablespoons flour
1½ cups beef stock, heated
½ cup dry red wine or dry sherry

Melt butter in a saucepan over low heat, add mushrooms and cook, stirring, for about 10 minutes. Stir in flour. When blended add heated stock and stir until smooth. Add wine or sherry and continue to cook, stirring until sauce is thick.

Makes about 2 cups of sauce.

Roll dough out on a lightly floured board as thinly as possible and cut into 3-inch squares. Place a scant teaspoon of filling on each square, moisten edges with water, and fold over to form a triangle. Moisten top edges with water then press together with fork to seal. Prick top with fork, place on a lightly buttered baking sheet and freeze until firm. Pack in plastic bags and seal. Store in freezer.

To serve: Place frozen turnovers on a greased baking sheet in preheated 400° oven and bake until lightly browned, about 30 minutes. Serve as a main course (3 to a serving) with mushroom sauce. You may also like to serve these as an appetizer without the mushroom sauce.

3

Grounds for Freezing

Meatballs can be gourmet fare, as the Italians have always known, and these two recipes are just that. The secret is in the meat, bread crumb and seasoning mixture and, of course, in the easy-to-make sauces. These are "double ups"—tonight's dinner and dinner for next week or next month, tasting all the better for a stay in the cold.

BASIC MEATBALLS

3 tablespoons butter
½ cup minced onion
3 pounds ground lean beef (or 2 pounds ground beef,
    ½ pound lean veal, and ½ pound ground lean pork)
1 cup fine dry bread crumbs
2 teaspoons salt
⅓ cup of one of the following:
    Heavy cream
    Evaporated milk
    Tomato sauce
    egg yolk blended with ¼ cup milk

Melt butter in a small skillet, add onion and sauté until limp. Scrape contents of skillet over meat in a large bowl, add remaining ingredients and mix all together thoroughly. Shape into small meatballs, using about 4 tablespoons of meat mixture for each.

Makes about three dozen.

To brown meatballs: Place meatballs, not touching, in a single layer in the bottom of a lightly greased broiler pan. Bake at 400°, turning each several times, until lightly browned on all sides (or brown meatballs in butter on top of stove in heavy skillet). Continue cooking in the sauce of your choice or place, not touching, in a single layer on a long, flat baking sheet. Place in freezer and freeze until firm. Remove baking sheet and store meatballs in sealed plastic bag in freezer. You can also freeze meatballs raw, or cooked and then frozen in sauce or plain stock.

Prepare a double batch and brown one part to cook in a sauce to serve now. Freeze the remainder without cooking. To serve, drop them, still frozen, into a different sauce for a totally different-tasting dish.

MEATBALLS with OLD-FASHIONED BROWN GRAVY

2½ cups beef stock
 8 frozen browned meatballs (see basic recipe, p. 49)
 3 tablespoons butter
 2 tablespoons minced onion
 ½ teaspoon minced garlic
 2 tablespoons flour
 ¼ cup (bottled) Kitchen Bouquet
 1 teaspoon Beau Monde seasoning (optional)
    Salt
    Pepper

Heat stock to simmering in a large and deep heavy skillet. Add frozen meatballs, a few at a time, so that stock continues to simmer. When all are added, let simmer for about 30 minutes or until balls are cooked through center. You can test one by gently piercing it with a small, sharp knife. The knife will go through to the center easily if the meat is cooked through. Remove meatballs with a slotted spoon and set aside. Reserve stock. In a second skillet melt butter over low heat. Add onions and garlic and cook until limp. Stir in flour. When blended, stir in stock, Kitchen Bouquet and Beau Monde seasoning. Add salt and pepper to taste. Cook, stirring, until sauce thickens. Place balls in oven-to-table casserole, pour sauce over them and bake in preheated 350° oven until bubbly hot. Serve from casserole.

Serves 4.

QUICK and EASY MEATBALLS in ITALIAN SAUCE

1 1-pound can Italian tomato sauce
¼ teaspoon mixed Italian herbs
½ cup dry red wine
8 frozen browned meatballs (see basic recipe, p. 49)

Combine sauce, herbs and wine in a large deep skillet. Bring to a simmer. Add frozen meatballs a few at a time so that sauce continues to simmer. Simmer over low heat until meatballs are cooked through center—about 30 minutes. These go great with any pasta.

Serves 4.

MEATBALLS with MARINARA SAUCE

1½ cups beef stock
8 raw frozen meatballs (see basic recipe, p. 49)
1 15½-ounce jar marinara sauce
¼ cup grated Parmesan cheese
   Salt
   Pepper
1 teaspoon oregano, crumbled (optional)

Heat stock to simmering in a large skillet. Add frozen meat-balls, a few at a time so that stock continues to simmer. Cook over low heat until meatballs are done through center, about 30 minutes. Remove them from the stock with a slotted spoon and place in oven-to-table casserole. Add marinara sauce and grated cheese to stock. Cook, stirring often, until cheese is melted and sauce thick and smooth. Season with salt and pepper. Add oregano, if desired. Pour over meatballs and bake in preheated 400° oven until very hot. Serve from casserole. Serves 4.

MEATBALLS in BLACK BEAN SAUCE

1½ cups beef stock
 8 browned frozen meatballs (see basic recipe, p. 49)
 1 10½-ounce can black bean soup
 ¼ cup dry sherry
 ½ teaspoon Beau Monde seasoning (optional)
    Salt
    Pepper
 2 tablespoons butter kneaded into 1 teaspoon flour (beurre manié)

Heat beef stock to simmering in a large and deep heavy skillet. Add meatballs a few at a time so that stock continues to simmer. Let simmer until meat is cooked through center, about 30 minutes. Remove balls with a slotted spoon and place in oven-to-table casserole. Add soup, sherry and seasoning to stock. Bring to boil, lower heat to simmer. Add beurre manié (butter-flour ball) and stir until it has dissolved and sauce has thickened. Correct seasoning with salt and pepper. Pour over meatballs and bake in preheated 400° oven until very hot. Serve from casserole with crusty French bread.
Serves 4 to 6.

MEATBALLS alla ROMANA

 6 slices white bread, crust removed
 ½ cup milk
 1 pound ground lean beef

½ pound ground fresh pork
2 tablespoons butter
1 large Italian purple onion, peeled and chopped
½ teaspoon mixed Italian herbs
2 eggs
1 teaspoon salt
½ teaspoon freshly ground black pepper
1 cup dry red wine
2 cups beef stock
3 cups water
1 6-ounce can tomato paste

Place bread in a large mixing bowl and add milk. Let stand until milk is absorbed. Add meats. Melt butter in a small skillet. Add onion and herbs. Sauté until onion is limp. Scrape entire contents of skillet over meat mixture. Add eggs, salt and pepper. Knead until well blended and very smooth. Let stand about 1 hour. Shape meat mixture into small balls and place them in a large, well-greased roasting pan. Bake at 450° until balls are lightly browned, turning them several times as they bake to brown evenly on all sides. Combine remaining ingredients in a large saucepan and stir over low heat until bubbly hot, thick and smooth. Place portion of meatballs to be frozen in a long, shallow freezer-to-oven-to-table baking dish and spoon some of the sauce over them. Cover and wrap in heavy-duty freezer foil. Label, date and freeze. Add remaining meatballs to sauce and let simmer over low heat for about 30 minutes. Serve over pasta or rice.

To serve frozen portion: Remove freezer wrap, cover and bake at 400° for 30 minutes. Uncover, fork-stir and continue to bake until bubbly hot. Serve with crusty Italian bread.

Serves 8.

MEATBALLS BURGUNDY

 2 tablespoons butter
 2 tablespoons onion, minced
 2 tablespoons green pepper, chopped
 2 pounds ground beef
 1 cup seasoned Italian bread crumbs
 2 teaspoons salt
⅛ teaspoon pepper
 2 eggs, slightly beaten
 4 tablespoons cold water
¼ cup corn oil
 2 cloves garlic
 1 large ripe tomato, chopped
 6 small white onions, peeled
12 small or 6 large mushrooms, coarsely chopped
 1 cup beef broth
 1 cup Burgundy wine
⅛ cup chopped parsley

Sauté onion and green pepper in butter until limp. Cool slightly, add to meat in mixing bowl. Add bread crumbs, salt, pepper, eggs and water. Form into small balls. Heat oil in skillet with garlic. Remove garlic, add meatballs a few at a time and brown well on all sides. Pour off oil from skillet, add remaining ingredients and browned meatballs. Bring to a boil. Simmer gently for 30 minutes. Cool, transfer portion for "now" use to a casserole and bake for 30 minutes at 350°. Put freezer portion in a freezer-to-oven casserole, wrap and freeze.

To serve freezer portion: Unwrap and bake, covered, for 1 hour in 400° oven. Add additional wine or water if needed.

Total recipe serves 8 to 12.

Serve meatballs Burgundy with flat noodles that have been cooked according to package directions, drained and tossed with 1 teaspoon of butter plus ¼ cup each of dry cottage cheese and Parmesan cheese. Add a few poppy seeds for extra flavor.

Start your meal with crisp celery stalks and thin-sliced raw turnips and carrots. End with fresh fruit topped with a smooth cream sauce from your freezer. This makes a well-balanced meal without cooking any extra vegetables.

MEATBALLS STROGANOFF (for tonight)
and
MEATBALLS in ITALIAN TOMATO SAUCE for PASTA
(for the freezer)

For the Meatballs

    9 slices white bread, crust removed
    ½ cup milk
    1 egg, lightly beaten
    2½ pounds ground beef
    ½ pound ground veal
    ½ teaspoon salt
    ¼ teaspoon pepper
       Vegetable oil
    3 tablespoons butter
    ¼ cup onion, minced

Place bread in a large mixing bowl, add milk and let stand until milk is absorbed. Add egg, meats, salt and pepper. Blend thoroughly. Let stand for about 1 hour, then shape into small balls. Brown the balls, a few at a time, in a little oil in a heavy skillet. Remove as browned. Place half in a freezer-to-oven baking dish, set remainder aside and keep warm.

For the Stroganoff

½ pound mushrooms, trimmed and sliced
2 tablespoons flour
1½ cups beef stock
1 tablespoon tomato paste
1 cup sour cream
1 pound flat noodles, cooked according to package
   directions

Wipe any remaining oil from skillet with a paper towel and add the butter. When melted add the onions and mushrooms. Sauté for about 5 minutes, then stir in the flour. Add the beef stock and tomato paste. Cook until smooth and bubbly. Return the warm meatballs and simmer for 10 minutes. Stir in the sour cream and heat without boiling. Serve over noodles.

For the Meatballs in Italian Tomato Sauce

2 8-ounce cans tomato sauce
¼ teaspoon mixed Italian herbs
½ cup dry red wine
2 tablespoons grated Parmesan cheese
1 pound thin spaghetti, cooked according to package
   directions

Combine tomato sauce, herbs and wine in a saucepan over medium heat. Bring to a boil, lower heat and let simmer for about 5 minutes. Add cheese and stir until melted. Pour over meatballs in baking dish. Wrap and freeze.

To serve: Unwrap. Bake, covered, in preheated 400° oven

for 40 minutes. Uncover and continue to bake until bubbly hot.
Serve over spaghetti.

Each dish serves 4 to 6.

MEAT CAKES with RED WINE SAUCE (for now)
and
CALIFORNIA BURGERS (for the freezer)

Tired of hamburger? You won't be after you've tried this
double recipe. Serve the meat cakes with red wine sauce with a
salad of avocado and onion slices, add garlic French bread and a
fruit dessert. The California burgers are a meal in themselves.

Basic Meat Cakes

2 medium-sized onions, chopped
4 tablespoons butter
2 teaspoons dry mustard
1 teaspoon salt
¼ teaspoon Worcestershire sauce
2 to 3 drops Tabasco sauce
3 pounds ground beef
2 eggs, slightly beaten

In a large skillet sauté onion in three tablespoons of butter
until limp. Turn off heat, add mustard, salt, Worcestershire
sauce, Tabasco and beef. Blend, then add eggs and mix
thoroughly. Shape into 12 cakes, about ½ inch thick and 4
inches in diameter. Place 6 cakes on a cookie sheet and freeze
until firm. When frozen place in plastic bag. Seal and store in
freezer

For the Meat Cakes with Red Wine Sauce

¼ teaspoon mixed Italian herbs
1 8-ounce can tomato sauce
¼ cup red wine
¼ cup water
3 tablespoons grated Parmesan cheese

Heat remaining butter in a large heavy skillet and brown meat cakes quickly on both sides. Add herbs, tomato sauce, wine and water. Partially cover skillet and let simmer for about 30 minutes. Place meat cakes on serving plates. Spoon sauce over them, sprinkle with Parmesan cheese and serve at once.
Serves 6.

For the California Burgers

2 tablespoons oil
3 English muffins, split and toasted
6 thick slices tomato
1 medium-sized avocado, peeled and cut into 12 wedges
2 cups shredded lettuce
2 cups chili sauce (see recipe, p. 59), heated
1 cup grated Cheddar cheese

Heat in a heavy skillet, add meat and cook covered for 5 minutes. Turn, cook an additional 5 minutes. Uncover and continue to cook 3 to 5 minutes on each side or until done to your taste. Place each meat cake on a half of a toasted English muffin, top with a tomato slice, then two avocado wedges. Cover with shredded lettuce and grated Cheddar cheese. Serve with chili sauce.
Serves 6.

Chili Sauce

This is a sauce to keep ready in the freezer, not only for California Burgers but to use any time you want a spicy, rich meat sauce. Great over frankfurters or served with noodles and grated cheese, or in any number of casseroles and such.

    4 strips bacon, cut into 1-inch pieces
    ¼ cup chopped onion
    ½ cup chopped green pepper
    2 pounds ground chuck
    2 1-pound cans tomatoes
    2 tablespoons white wine vinegar
    1 teaspoon sugar
    1 teaspoon salt
    ¼ teaspoon black pepper
    ½ small clove garlic, chopped
    1 to 2 tablespoons chili powder
    1 6-ounce can tomato puree
    2 cups water

Cook bacon, onion and green pepper in heavy deep skillet over low heat until onions are transparent and pepper is limp. Add meat, cook, stirring frequently, until well browned. Add remaining ingredients. Simmer slowly for 1 hour, stirring frequently. Pour into second pan to cook quickly. Pour into 2-cup containers, wrap and freeze.

To use: Heat slowly in top half of double boiler over simmering water until thawed and bubbly hot.

I've served this chili corn casserole at innumerable supper parties and I've never had a scrap left over. It's extra simple to make and keep ready in the freezer for the next time you would like to have a few people over, and at the same time you'll be making a wonderful hot chili to have for now or to freeze as you like. I like chili served fiery hot with plenty of crisp crackers and I finish up with a big bowl of cut-up fresh fruit, well laced with kirsch and sugar. Add plenty of black coffee, some crisp cookies and I don't think you'll have complaints from anyone.

As always this recipe is planned for easy step-by-step preparation, the freezer casserole is completed and stored away, then the finishing touches are added to the chili for now. If you prefer both casseroles may be frozen for future serving. Either one can, of course, be served without freezing.

CHILI CORN CASSEROLE (for the freezer)
and
CHILI CON CARNE (to serve now)

This easy recipe allows you to slip in a casserole for the freezer while you whip up a batch of chili. Incidentally chili freezes well, too, so if there are any leftovers, pour into containers, wrap and freeze.

Chili Base

3 pounds ground beef
2 large onions, minced
2 cloves garlic, minced
2 tablespoons mild oil

2 to 4 tablespoons chili powder (depending on how you like your chili)
1 16-ounce can tomatoes
1 6-ounce can tomato paste
1 cup beef stock or water
1½ teaspoons salt

In a large heavy pot sauté the beef, onion and garlic in the oil over low heat until meat is no longer pink. Stir in chili powder, add tomatoes, tomato paste, stock and salt. Let simmer about 30 minutes. Add additional water if chili becomes too thick.

For the Corn Casserole

1 14-ounce can whole kernel corn
1 12-ounce package frozen lima beans (sufficiently thawed to separate beans)
1 4-ounce package corn chips
½ cup shredded sharp Cheddar cheese

Spoon half of chili into a freezer-to-oven casserole. Stir in corn and lima beans. Cover and wrap in heavy-duty foil, label, date and freeze.

For the Chili Con Carne

To remaining chili add cumin, kidney beans and beef stock, simmer another 30 minutes before serving.
Serves 6.

To serve the freezer casserole: Remove freezer wrap and cover with regular foil. Place in cold oven. Set temperature at 400° and bake for 1 hour. Uncover, add kidney beans and

fork-stir to blend. Continue until heated through. Remove from oven and stir in corn chips and cheese. Serve from casserole.
Serves 6.

Not meat loaf again! But these are no ordinary meat loaves. A brown sugar glaze on one takes it right out of the ordinary, chili sauce transforms another and the country meat loaves with two quick sauces have a deep-down good flavor that makes you hope there will be leftovers for lunch.

MEAT LOAF with BROWN SUGAR GLAZE
(to serve now)
and
CHILI MEAT LOAF (for the freezer)

    1 cup soft bread crumbs
    ¾ cup milk or tomato juice
    1 tablespoon butter
    ¼ cup minced onion
    2 pounds ground beef
    1 teaspoon seasoned salt
    ¼ teaspoon pepper
       Flour
    2 slices bacon
       Brown sugar glaze
       Bottled chili sauce

Put bread crumbs in mixing bowl and add milk or tomato juice. Let stand 10 to 15 minutes. Melt butter in a small skillet. Add onion and sauté until limp. Add to bread and milk, add beef and seasoning. Mix thoroughly. Shape into two equal loaves. Dredge each loaf lightly with flour and place in a lightly greased shallow baking dish. Arrange 1 bacon slice over each and place in preheated 350° oven.

Freezer portion: Remove one loaf after 40 minutes (transfer the bacon to the second loaf). Cool slightly. Wrap and freeze.

To serve unfrozen portion: Continue to bake for an additional 30 minutes. For the last 15 minutes of baking, remove bacon and baste with glaze.

To serve frozen loaf: Put foil-wrapped frozen loaf in a shallow baking dish and bake at 350° for 1 hour. Remove foil and continue to bake for 15 minutes, basting with chili sauce.

Brown Sugar Glaze

  1 teaspoon cider vinegar
½ cup catsup
⅓ cup brown sugar
  1 teaspoon dry mustard

Combine ingredients and spread over meat loaf for last 30 minutes of baking.

COUNTRY MEAT LOAVES with Quick Tomato Sauce
and
COUNTRY MEAT LOAVES with Deviled Sauce

Meat loaves

3 large baking potatoes, peeled and coarsely chopped
1 large mild onion, coarsely chopped
1 large tart apple, peeled, cored and coarsely chopped

 2 eggs
½ cup catsup
 2 pounds ground beef
½ pound bulk pork sausage meat
 1 teaspoon salt
¼ teaspoon pepper

Place half of potatoes, onion, apple, eggs and catsup in container of electric blender and blend to a thick puree. Remove to a mixing bowl and puree remaining half of ingredients. Combine puree with meats and seasoning. Mix thoroughly. Pack into two foil-lined lightly greased bread pans (9x5x3 inches) and cover both pans with foil. Bake at 350° for 1 hour. Remove one pan. Refrigerate until cold. Wrap and freeze.

To serve unfrozen portion: Continue to bake for 30 minutes. Unmold, slice and serve with quick tomato sauce (below).

To serve frozen portion: Bake at 375° for 1 hour. Remove foil and continue to bake for 30 to 40 minutes. Serve with Deviled Sauce (below).

Quick Tomato Sauce

 1 6-ounce can tomato paste
¼ cup brandy
    Hot water
    Sugar
    Garlic salt
    Freshly ground black pepper
    Tabasco sauce

Combine tomato paste and brandy in a saucepan. Place over low heat. Stir in sufficient hot water to make a smooth sauce. Add a sprinkling of sugar and season to taste with salt, garlic salt, pepper and Tabasco sauce.

Deviled Sauce

2 tablespoons butter
2 tablespoons flour
1 cup beef stock or broth, heated
2 tablespoons Sauce Diable
2 tablespoons dry sherry
  Seasoned salt
  Pepper

Melt butter in a saucepan over low heat and stir in flour. When blended add beef stock and stir with a whisk until smooth. Add Sauce Diable and sherry. Continue to stir until sauce thickens. Season to taste with seasoned salt and pepper.

INDIVIDUAL ORANGE-GLAZED MEAT LOAVES
and
INDIVIDUAL MEAT LOAVES with Barbecue Sauce

Here is a basic recipe for meat loaf with two different sauces. The loaves may be frozen for easy baking, but the barbecue sauce should be made at the last minute and spooned over the loaves just before serving. Needless to say, either version can be served "now."

Basic Meat Loaves

2 tablespoons butter
2 tablespoons minced onion

2 pounds ground lean beef
2½ cups soft crustless bread crumbs
2 eggs, beaten
1 teaspoon salt
½ teaspoon pepper

For the Glazed Meat Loaves

4 tablespoons dark brown sugar
1 teaspoon dry mustard
4 thin slices peeled, seeded orange

For the Barbecued Meat Loaves

1 cup catsup
1 tablespoon Worcestershire sauce
2 or 3 dashed Tabasco sauce
1 teaspoon cider vinegar
1 teaspoon light brown sugar

Sauté the onion in the butter until soft. Combine with remaining ingredients listed under basic meat loaves (above) and blend thoroughly.

For glazed meat loaves: Lightly butter four individual freezer-to-oven round baking dishes. Sprinkle the bottoms and sides evenly with the sugar and mustard. Lay a slice of orange in the botton of each and fill each with meat loaf mixture. Wrap each dish and freeze or bake in preheated 350° oven for 45 minutes.

For the meat loaves with barbecue sauce: Lightly butter four individual ramekins and pack with meat mixture. Wrap and freeze or bake in a preheated 350° oven for 45 minutes. Prepare sauce during the last few minutes of baking; combine remaining ingredients in a saucepan and heat to steamy hot. Unmold meat loaves onto serving plates and spoon sauce over each. Serves 4.

To bake frozen meat loaves: Uncover and bake in a preheated 350° oven for 1 hour. Remove from oven and let stand on a cake rack for 10 minutes before unmolding. Serves 4.

I love casserole dinners. Easy to make and even easier to serve, they need only the addition of an antipasto (for an Italian flavor) or a salad plus good hard rolls and a dessert. Nothing to it. Even simpler if the casserole is already prepared and in the freezer ready for a really good, quick but effortless meal.

GROUND BEEF and ZUCCHINI CASSEROLE
(for tonight)
(and, while you're at it),
BEEF and BEANS (for the freezer)

3 tablespoons butter
½ cup chopped onion
2 pounds lean ground beef
1 6-ounce can chopped mushrooms
3 cups beef stock
1 1-pound, 3-ounce can Italian-style tomatoes
½ 6-ounce can tomato paste
1 teaspoon salt
½ teaspoon pepper
½ teaspoon mixed Italian herbs
1 can (15½ ounces) kidney beans, drained and rinsed
4 medium-sized zucchini, trimmed and sliced
1 1-pound package flat noodles, cooked according to package directions
Parmesan cheese, grated

Melt the butter in a large heavy skillet. In it sauté the onions until limp. Add the meat and fork-stir until no longer pink. Add mushrooms, stock, tomatoes and tomato paste. Season with salt, pepper and herbs. Partially cover and let simmer for about 30 minutes. Add a little water if sauce becomes too thick. Transfer portion to be frozen to a freezer-to-oven baking dish. Add beans and fork-stir to blend. Wrap and freeze. Add zucchini to portion to be served without freezing. Let simmer until zucchini are tender but still a bit crisp. Serve over flat noodles and sprinkle each serving with Parmesan cheese.

To serve frozen casserole: Unwrap and cover casserole and bake in preheated 400° oven for 30 minutes. Uncover, fork-stir and continue to bake until bubbly hot.

Each dish serves 6 to 8.

RUSSIAN BEEF with NOODLES and SOUR CREAM

1½ pounds lean beef
⅓ cup flour mixed with ½ teaspoon salt and ¼ teaspoon pepper
2 to 3 tablespoons vegetable oil
2 tablespoons butter
1 large mild purple onion, chopped
1 cup beef stock
¼ cup dry vermouth or white wine
½ teaspoon thyme
1 can (6 ounces) chopped mushrooms and liquid
1 1-pound package flat noodles, cooked according to package directions
1 1 cup sour cream

Cut meat into thin, narrow strips. Dredge in flour. Using a large skillet, brown meat, about one half at a time, in hot oil. Remove with a spatula as browned and let drain on paper toweling. Add the butter and in it sauté the onion until limp. Return meat to skillet. Add stock and wine and thyme. Cover and let simmer for about 45 minutes or until meat is tender. Add mushrooms and cook 5 minutes. Add noodles and fork-stir until blended. Spoon into two shallow freezer-to-oven baking dishes. Wrap and freeze one casserole. Place second in preheated 375° oven for 15 to 20 minutes, or until very hot. Serve from the casserole.

To serve frozen casserole: Remove freezer wrap. Cover and place in a preheated 400° oven for 30 minutes. Uncover, fork-stir and bake until thoroughly heated.

Each dish serves 4.

TWO BEEF and MACARONI CASSEROLES

This is a double-up recipe, each to serve four—one for now, one for the freezer, or freeze both for a buffet supper party.

¼ cup butter
1 small purple onion, minced
1 clove garlic, minced
1½ pounds ground lean beef
1 6-ounce package mushrooms, sliced
2 cups beef stock
1 1-pound, 3-ounce can Italian-style tomatoes
1 can (6 ounces) tomato paste
1 teaspoon salt
½ teaspoon freshly ground black pepper
1 teaspoon mixed Italian herbs
1 1-pound package small elbow macaroni
 Vegetable oil
 Salt
1 10-ounce package frozen peas, sufficiently thawed to
 separate peas

1 tablespoon butter
½ cup soft fresh bread crumbs
¼ cup grated Parmesan cheese

Melt the butter in a large heavy skillet, add onion and garlic. Sauté until limp. Add meat and cook, stirring, until it is no longer pink. Add the mushrooms, stock, tomatoes and tomato paste. Blend, then add salt, pepper and herbs. Bring mixture to a boil, lower heat and let simmer very gently for about 1 hour. Add a little water if mixture becomes too thick. Remove from heat. Cook macaroni until just tender in a large pot of lightly salted boiling water to which you have added 1 teaspoon vegetable oil. Drain. Add macaroni and peas to meat mixture. Spoon the whole into two freezer casseroles. Melt the 1 tablespoon butter in a small skillet. Remove from heat, stir in bread crumbs and grated cheese. Top each casserole with mixture. Cover and wrap in freezer foil. Label, date and freeze.

To serve: Remove freezer foil and cover with regular foil. Bake at 400° for 1 hour, uncover and bake until bubbly hot and topping is lightly browned (about 30 minutes).

Each casserole serves 4.

4

Some Budget-Minded
Main Dishes

If you think of lamb, veal and pork only as expensive chops and roasts, think again. Here's a collection of recipes that use the more inexpensive cuts with even more interesting and flavorful results plus some meatless main dishes and a couple that make use of leftovers.

RATATOUILLE
and
LAMB BOHEMIENNE

Make a beautiful beginning to dinner or a light luncheon dish with a classic ratatouille and go on to the lamb Bohemienne for the freezer.

Basic Recipe

3 small eggplants (about 3 pounds)
  Salt
2 tablespoons olive oil
1 large mild onion, chopped
2 cloves garlic, minced
1 small green pepper, seeded and chopped
1 teaspoon flour
2 1-pound cans Italian-style tomatoes
  1-ounce can anchovy fillets
  Freshly ground black pepper

For the Ratatouille

Lettuce
Pimento-stuffed green olives

For the Lamb Bohémienne

2 cups chopped lean leftover cooked lamb
½ cup fine dry bread crumbs
2 tablespoons melted butter

For the ratatouille: Peel eggplant. Cut into cubes. Place in a colander and sprinkle with salt. Let stand 30 to 45 minutes to drain. Rinse under cold water, blot dry with paper toweling. Heat oil in a large heavy pot. Add onion, garlic and green pepper, and sauté until limp. Sprinkle with flour and stir to blend. Add tomatoes and oil from anchovy fillets. Chop and add anchovies. Let simmer over low heat until mixture is very thick. Season to taste with salt and pepper. Line a salad bowl with lettuce. Spoon in about half of ratatouille. Refrigerate until well chilled. Garnish with olives before serving as an appetizer or luncheon main course salad. Great with crusty French bread.

Serves 4 to 6.

For the lamb Bohémienne: Cover the bottom of a freezer-to-oven baking dish with remaining ratatouille. Add a layer of lamb and cover with ratatouille. Mix bread crumbs with melted butter and sprinkle over surface of dish. Wrap and freeze.

To serve: Remove freezer wrap. Cover dish with foil. Bake in preheated 400° oven for 45 minutes. Uncover and continue to bake until heated through.

Serves 4.

VEAL STEW
and
VEAL RAGOUT

Basic Recipe

4 tablespoons flour
2 teaspoons salt

3 pounds lean boneless veal, cut into 1¼-inch cubes
4 tablespoons vegetable oil
1 can condensed chicken broth
1 1-pound can tomatoes
2 tablespoons tomato paste
½ pound fresh mushrooms, trimmed and sliced
12 very small white onions, peeled
4 carrots, scraped and cut into ½-inch slices

For Veal Ragout

Mix flour with salt. Roll veal cubes in mixture. Shake off excess. Heat about 2 tablespoons of the oil in a large heavy skillet. In it brown veal cubes, a few at a time, adding more oil as needed. Remove cubes as browned and set aside. Pour fat from skillet. Return veal cubes to it, add chicken stock and tomatoes. Sir in tomato paste. Partially cover pot and let simmer until cubes can be easily pierced with a small sharp knife. Add mushrooms, onions and carrots and continue to cook until meat can be easily pierced with a fork. Transfer portion to be frozen to a freezer-to-oven-to-table baking dish. Wrap and freeze. Cook portion to be served until meat and vegetables are tender.

Serves 4 to 6.

To serve frozen portion: Remove freezer wrap. Place in preheated 400° oven and bake, covered, for about 45 minutes. Uncover, fork-stir and bake until bubbly hot. Add partially thawed peas last 10 minutes of baking. Serve over white rice.

Each serves 4 to 6.

IRISH LAMB STEW (for now)
and
LAMB with KIDNEY BEAN CASSEROLE
(for the freezer)

Basic Recipe

3 pounds lean lamb shoulder, cut into 1-inch cubes
3 tablespoons flour
  Oil for browning
2 tablespoons butter
1 tablespoon sugar
1 teaspoon salt
¼ teaspoon pepper
4 cups beef or chicken stock or broth
2 cloves garlic, peeled
¼ teaspoon thyme
1 bay leaf

For Irish Lamb Stew

8 to 12 small white onions, peeled
8 to 12 small new potatoes, peeled (or 2 to 3 large baking
  potatoes, peeled and quartered)

For Lamb with Kidney Bean Casserole

1 1-pound can red kidney beans (drained)
1 10-ounce package frozen cut green beans

Dredge meat with flour and shake off excess, reserving excess flour. Brown, a few pieces at a time, in a small amount of hot oil, removing each piece as browned. When all are browned, pour any remaining oil from pot, wipe, and return all of the meat cubes to it. Add the butter and fork-stir until melted. Sprinkle with the sugar and reserved flour. Cook, covered, over low heat for about 1 minute. Season with salt and pepper. Add stock, garlic, thyme and bay leaf. Cover and let simmer over low heat until lamb is almost tender. Remove and discard bay leaf and garlic. Remove the meat with a slotted spoon and divide it between two casseroles (one for the freezer). Cover equally with sauce. Add the onions and potatoes to one casserole. Cover and bake in 350° oven for 30 minutes or until potatoes, onions and meat are tender. Serve from the casserole. To the second casserole add the kidney beans and frozen green beans. Fork-stir to blend. Wrap and freeze. To serve, bake uncovered at 400° for 1 hour. Reduce heat to 325°, uncover, fork-stir and continue to bake until heated.

Each casserole serves 4 to 6.

PORK SOUTH AFRICAN STYLE

Make this dish with beans for the freezer, with rice for now.

1 cup dried white beans
2 pounds boneless lean fresh pork, cut in 1-inch cubes
6 tablespoons butter
1 large onion, chopped
1 teaspoon salt
½ teaspoon freshly ground black pepper
1 tablespoon curry powder

½ teaspoon dried red pepper flakes
2 cups chicken or beef stock
4 medium-sized fresh tomatoes, chopped
2 tablespoons vinegar
1 tablespoon sugar
2 medium-sized tart apples, peeled, cored and chopped
½ cup raisins
3 cups cooked white rice

Soak beans overnight in water to cover. Drain, place in a saucepan and cover with fresh water. Bring to a boil, lower heat and let simmer for about 1 hour, or until soft but not mushy. Drain and set aside for freezer dish. Trim fat from the pork and place the meat in a greased roasting pan in preheated 400° oven for about 30 minutes or until well browned, then drain. Melt the butter in a large heavy pot and add the onion. Sauté over medium heat until limp. Add the browned meat. Stir and add salt, pepper, curry powder and pepper flakes. Cook, stirring, a few seconds. Add stock, tomatoes, vinegar, sugar and apples. Partially cover and let simmer over low heat until pork is almost tender. Stir in raisins. Place beans in a long, shallow oven-to-freezer-to-table baking dish. Spoon portion of pork and sauce to be frozen over beans. Fork-stir to blend. Wrap and freeze. Simmer remaining stew until meat is fork tender. Spoon over rice and serve at once.

Serves 4 to 6.

To serve frozen portion: Unwrap and bake casserole covered for 1 hour in 400° oven. Uncover, fork-stir and continue to bake until bubbly hot.

Serves 4 to 6

ITALIAN VEAL SAUCE with MUSHROOMS and PROSCIUTTO
(to serve now over spaghetti)
and
RAGÙ ALLA BOLOGNESE with CREAM
(to freeze and serve over noodles)

Basic Recipe

3 tablespoons butter
½ cup minced onion
½ pound lean veal, ground twice
4 cups chicken stock
1 cup dry white wine
1 teaspoon salt
¼ teaspoon freshly ground black pepper
4 tablespoons tomato paste
Additional stock for water if needed

For the Veal Sauce

½ teaspoon freshly grated lemon rind
1 4-ounce can sliced mushrooms
¼ pound prosciutto or lean ham, minced
1 pound thin spaghetti, cooked according to package directions
Grated Parmesan cheese

For the Ragù

2 tablespoons butter
¼ pound chicken livers, chopped
½ cup heavy cream
1 pound flat noodles, cooked according to package
  directions
Grated Parmesan cheese

Melt butter in a large heavy pot. Add onion and veal. Cook, stirring until onion is limp, veal has turned color. Add stock, wine, salt, pepper and tomato paste. Stir until blended and bring to boil. Lower heat and simmer for about 1 hour. If sauce becomes too thick while cooking, add additional stock or water. Pour half of sauce into freezer container. Cool, wrap and freeze. To remaining sauce add lemon rind, mushrooms and prosciutto or ham. Cook, stirring, a final 10 to 15 minutes. Serve over just-cooked thin spaghetti. Sprinkle grated Parmesan cheese over each serving.

Serves 4 to 6.

To prepare frozen ragù: Unwrap and place container in a pan of warm (not hot) water until sufficiently thawed to transfer to the top of a double boiler over simmering water. Break up frozen block as it thaws. When thawed, stir until smooth and hot. Keep hot over simmering water. Melt butter in a small saucepan. Add chicken livers and sauté until no longer pink. Add to sauce, add cream and stir until heated. Serve over just-cooked noodles. Sprinkle each serving with grated Parmesan cheese.

Serves 4 to 6.

TEXAS BAKED BEANS (to enjoy now)
and
FRENCH CASSOULET (for the freezer)

2 pounds dried small navy beans
3 to 4 quarts water

For the Texas Baked Beans

2 cups bean water
½ teaspoon salt
3 tablespoons catsup
2 teaspoons chili powder
1 teaspoon dry mustard
¼ cup red wine vinegar
1 clove garlic, minced
1 large onion, chopped
¼ pound salt pork, washed free of loose salt, cut into
   1-inch cubes

For the Cassoulet

2 cups bean water
1 onion, chopped
1 clove garlic, minced
½ teaspoon leaf thyme
½ teaspoon salt
2 8-ounce cans tomato sauce
1 cup dry white wine
½ pound bulk sausage

1 to 2 cups leftover roast turkey, chunks of light and dark
  meat with crisp skin (or substitute any other leftover
  roasted or braised meat)
1 cup buttered bread crumbs

Bring beans and water to boil in a large heavy pot. Let cook a
few minutes, then stand for 1 hour. Partially cover and simmer
for 1 hour. Drain, saving bean water. Divide beans equally in
two casseroles (one for the freezer).

For the Texas baked beans: Combine the 2 cups bean water
with salt, catsup, chili powder, mustard and vinegar. Mix
thoroughly and pour over beans in casserole. There should be
sufficient liquid to come to top of beans. If not, add more bean
water. Add onion, garlic and salt pork and fork-stir them into
beans. Cover and bake in a 300° oven for about 3 hours, adding
additional bean water if needed to keep beans moist while
baking. Uncover last 30 minutes to brown surface of salt pork
cubes.

Serves 6.

For the cassoulet: Pour bean water over beans in freezer-to-
oven casserole now. Add onion, garlic, thyme, salt and fork-stir
to distribute evenly. Cover and bake in 300° oven for 1 hour.
Combine tomato sauce and wine. Add to beans and fork-stir to
blend. Cover and bake another hour. In a small skillet brown
the sausage and pour off the fat. Add it along with the turkey to
the beans and again fork-stir. Cover and wrap. Label, date and
freeze.

To serve: Remove freezer wrap. Bake, covered, in preheated 375° oven for 1 hour. Uncover, sprinkle bread crumbs
over surface. Reduce heat to 325° and continue to bake until
beans are tender and cassoulet is bubbly hot.

Serves 6 to 8

FRIED EGGPLANT (to enjoy now)
and
EGGPLANT MOZZARELLA (for the freezer)

3 medium-sized eggplants
  Salt
4 eggs
3 tablespoons milk
3 cups Italian-style bread crumbs

For the Fried Eggplant

Olive or corn oil—or a mixture of ½ corn oil, ½ olive oil

For the Eggplant Mozzarella

1 1-pound jar Italian cooking sauce
½ teaspoon mixed Italian herbs
½ pound mozzarella cheese, shredded

Peel the eggplants and cut into thin slices. Sprinkle each slice with salt and place in even stacks of 4 or 5 slices on two cake racks and cover with foil. Place a heavy weight over them—a heavy pot, top or plate—and let stand about 30 minutes to drain. Rinse off salt and pat slices dry. Beat eggs with milk in a small bowl; pour into a shallow dish. Place bread crumbs in a large plate. Dip eggplant slices first in egg mixture then in bread crumbs to coat each side.

For the fried eggplant: Cover the bottom of a large heavy skillet with oil and place over medium heat. Fry about ⅓ of the eggplant slices in a single layer, a few at a time, until browned on both sides. Remove as browned and drain on paper toweling. (May be kept warm on foil in a 200° oven for 20 to 25 minutes before serving.)

Serves 4 to 6.

For the eggplant mozzarella: Mix herbs into cooking sauce. Place alternate layers of eggplant, cooking sauce and cheese in a greased long, shallow freezer-to-oven baking dish. Cover with foil and bake in preheated oven for 25 minutes. Wrap in foil and freeze.

To serve: Unwrap heavy-duty foil. Bake, covered in a preheated 400° oven for 40 minutes. Uncover and continue to bake until heated through.

Serves 6.

CASEROLE de FLAGEOLETS
(Kidney Bean Casserole)

2 cups dried white kidney beans
8 cups water
1 clove garlic
1 onion stuck with 2 cloves
1 bay leaf
¼ pound boiled or baked ham, diced
4 tablespoons olive oil
½ cup chopped onions
½ cup chopped green pepper
2 cups solid-pack tomatoes (#2 can)
1 teaspoon salt
1 teaspoon pepper
½ teaspoon thyme
¼ cup dry sherry

Soak beans overnight, drain, add water, garlic, onion, bay leaf and ham. Simmer gently until beans are tender—about 3 hours. Heat olive oil in saucepan, add onions and green pepper. Sauté until limp. Add tomatoes, salt, pepper, and thyme and simmer 15 minutes.* Combine sauce and beans in casserole. Cool, wrap and freeze.

To serve: Bake in covered casserole at 350° until thoroughly hot, stir in sherry and serve. French bread goes well with this dish, as does a good green salad. Finish the meal with fresh fruit and cheese and a glass of red wine.

Serves 6 to 8.

For a summer night's supper there's nothing nicer than a salad, but it needs to be substantial. This one is and needs only the addition of some sliced ripe tomatoes in a vinaigrette sauce plus, perhaps, a deep-dish peach pie for a truly delicious meal. Your bonus: a main dish casserole to take from the freezer for a fast oven-to-table dinner.

BEAN SALAD with TUNA FISH (to enjoy now)
and
WHITE BEANS for TOMATO and HAM CASSEROLE
(for the freezer)

2 pounds dried white kidney beans

Put the beans in a large heavy pot. Cover with cold water. Bring to a boil and boil for 2 minutes. Remove from heat and let stand for 1 hour. Again bring to a boil, then lower heat and let

*To serve without freezing, transfer sauce and beans to casserole, stir in sherry and serve.

simmer uncovered until beans are tender—about 1½ hours. (Add more water if needed to keep them well covered as they cook.) Drain into colander.

For the Salad

⅓ cup mild salad oil
2 tablespoons cider vinegar
½ teaspoon salt
1 7-ounce can tuna fish
⅓ cup minced parsley
   Pitted ripe olives

For the Casserole

2 tablespoons mild oil
1 clove garlic, peeled and finely minced
1 teaspoon mixed Italian herbs
1 large ripe tomato, peeled and chopped
1 cup large ripe tomato, peeled and chopped
1 cup chopped lean ham
2 tablespoons tomato paste
1 1-pound can tomatoes
   Salt
   Pepper
1 tablespoon cider vinegar

To prepare salad: Combine oil, vinegar and salt in salad bowl. Beat with whisk until blended. Add half of the still warm beans. Break up tuna and add with its oil. Fork-stir, cover and set aside 1 to 2 hours to absorb flavors. Add additional salt, if needed, and chill if desired. Add parsley, fork-stir and garnish with ripe olives.

Serves 6

To prepare casserole: Heat the olive oil in the same pot in which the beans were cooked. Add garlic and herbs. Sauté until garlic is limp. Add the ripe tomato and ham. Cook, stirring often, until tomato is soft. Stir in tomato paste and canned tomatoes. Bring to boil. Remove from heat and add beans. Gently fork-stir to blend. Season with salt and pepper. Stir in vinegar.

To freeze: Transfer to one or two fairly shallow oven-to-table baking dishes. Wrap and freeze.

To serve: Unwrap freezer foil and cover baking dish with regular foil. Bake at 400° for 30 minutes. Uncover, fork-stir and continue to bake until heated through.

Serves 6.

BAKED MAC with THREE CHEESES ith Three Cheeses

1 pound macaroni
3 tablespoons butter
2 tablespoons flour
2½ cups milk
1 egg, lightly beaten
½ teaspoon salt
½ teaspoon pepper
½ cup grated Gruyère or Swiss cheese
½ cup grated Parmesan cheese
½ cup grated fontina or mozzarella cheese
½ cup buttered bread crumbs

Cook macaroni in large quantity of boiling water until done but still firm. Drain, rinse with cold water, and drain again. Melt butter in saucepan. When bubbly add flour, stir until well blended. Slowly add milk. Cook, stirring frequently, until sauce begins to thicken. Remove from fire, cool slightly, blend in egg, salt, and pepper. Place macaroni in well-buttered casserole, stir in cheeses first, then sauce. Sprinkle with bread crumbs, cool slightly, wrap and freeze. For cook's night out, tell your spouse to remove casserole from freezer and bake, covered, in a 400° oven for 45 to 50 minutes. Uncover and bake 5 minutes longer to brown crumb topping.

5

Various Chicken Recipes

Chicken is such a good buy I like to serve it often, but one does get tired of the same old broiled, baked or fried versions. Add a little glamour to your repertoire of chicken recipes with these versions that I've borrowed, begged and stolen from some of the best cooks in the business. The frozen dishes are especially good. Maybe it's because it's so wonderfully satisfying to have such great food on hand ready only for the heating.

CHICKEN CURRY (to enjoy now)
and
CURRY SAUCE (for the freezer)

Basic Recipe

¼ pound butter
1 medium-sized mild onion, minced
2 medium-sized crisp, tart apples, peeled, seeded, cored
   and very finely minced
1 to 2 tablespoons curry powder to taste
½ teaspoon salt
¼ cup flour
3 cups chicken stock, heated
1 cup milk at room temperature

For the Chicken Curry

2 egg yolks, lightly beaten
½ cup dry white wine, at room temperature
3 cups cooked chicken, skinned, boned and cut into large dice
3 cups cooked white rice

For the Curry Sauce

¼ cup dry sherry
½ cup sour cream

Melt butter in a large heavy pot. In it sauté onion and apple until apple is sufficiently soft to mash easily with a fork. Stir in curry powder, salt and flour. When blended add stock and milk. Simmer over very low heat for about 15 minutes. Pour half of sauce into a freezer container. Cook, wrap and freeze.

For the chicken curry: Add wine to beaten egg yolks and beat until blended. Add to sauce, stirring vigorously as added. Cook, stirring, until sauce is very thick and smooth. Add chicken and cook, stirring, until it is heated. Serve over rice and offer an assortment of accompaniments.

To use frozen curry sauce: Unwrap container and place it in a shallow pan of warm (not hot) water until the contents can be easily released into the top half of a double boiler over simmering water. As it heats, break up sauce with a fork. When it is a liquid, beat with whisk until smooth. Add sherry and continue to stir until heated. Stir in sour cream, then add 2 to 3 cups of any of the following:

    Cooked chopped shrimp or any other seafood
    Cooked leftover diced turkey or chicken
    Cooked leftover cubed lamb, pork or ham
Serve with rice and offer a variety of accompaniments or top dish with fresh steamed asparagus or broccoli.

Curry Accompaniments (Serve 3 or more)

Chopped dry-roasted peanuts or slivered toasted almonds
Shredded coconut
Minced green onion
Raisins or currants, plumped in a little sherry or brandy
Mango Chutney (always)

A YANKEE PAELLA (to serve now)
and
CHICKEN ITALIAN (for the freezer)

2 2½ to 3-pound frying chickens, cut into serving pieces
½ cup corn oil
   Salt
   Pepper

For the Chicken Italian

1 1-pound can Italian-style tomatoes with basil
2 tablespoons dry sherry
2 tablespoons tomato paste
½ teaspoon mixed Italian herbs
2 fresh tomatoes, coarsely chopped

For the Paella

2 medium-sized onions, chopped
1 medium-sized green pepper, chopped
1 clove garlic, chopped
2 cups uncooked long-grain rice
1 8-ounce can tomato sauce
2 10¾-ounce cans chicken broth
1 cup water
½ teaspoon cumin
¼ teaspoon powdered saffron
½ pound cooked shrimp, peeled and deveined
   Ripe olives
   Pimentos

In a heavy skillet, over medium-high heat, sauté the chicken pieces in the oil until golden brown. When all are browned, sprinkle with salt and pepper.

To prepare the chicken Italian: Place half of the chicken pieces in a single layer in a long, shallow freezer-to-oven baking dish. Combine canned tomatoes with basil, sherry, tomato paste and herbs. Stir until well blended. Pour over chicken pieces, add fresh tomatoes to dish. Place in preheated 350° oven and bake for thirty minutes. Cool slightly, cover, wrap and freeze.

To prepare the paella: Put onions, green pepper, garlic and rice in the skillet in which the chicken was cooked and cook, stirring until all cooking oil is absorbed. Remove chicken. Stir tomato sauce, chicken broth and water into the skillet. Add cumin and saffron. Arrange chicken pieces over rice. Bring to a boil. Cover and simmer 30 minutes. Stir in shrimp, cover and cook a final 10 minutes. Garnish with ripe olives and pimentos. Serve from the skillet.

To serve frozen chicken Italian: Unwrap and bake, covered, in preheated 400° oven for 45 minutes. Uncover, fork-stir and continue to bake until heated.

Both serve 6.

CHICKEN GUMBO
INDIVIDUAL SEAFOOD and CHICKEN GUMBO CAS-SEROLES

Chicken Gumbo

2 2½ to 3-pound chickens, each cut into 6 serving pieces
2 tablespoons butter

1 tablespoon oil
½ pound lean ham, chopped
1 large mild onion, chopped
1 10-ounce package frozen okra
4 1-pound cans tomatoes
2 teaspoons mixed Creole herbs or
2 quarts water
  Salt
  Freshly ground black pepper
2 teaspoons filé powder (optional)
  Cooked white rice

For Seafood Gumbo

1 pound raw shrimp, shelled and deveined
1 pint oysters and their liquid
  Crusty French or Italian bread

Wash chicken pieces and blot thoroughly dry. Heat the butter and oil in a large heavy stew pot. Add chicken pieces, cover and cook over medium heat for 10 minutes. Uncover, add ham, onion and okra. Stir-fry until onion is limp. Add tomatoes, herbs and sufficient water to cover ingredients completely (about 2 quarts). Season with salt and pepper. Partially cover pot and let cook over low heat until chicken is very tender. Remove 4 large pieces of chicken. Remove and discard skin and bones. Cut meat into "largish" pieces and place in freezer container. Cover with about 4 cups of the gumbo liquid. Cover, wrap and freeze. Remove remaining gumbo from heat and transfer to freezer-to-oven-to-table casserole, wrap and freeze. Or stir in about 1 teaspoon filé powder and serve immediately in deep soup bowls over mounds of just-cooked white rice.

To serve frozen casserole, unwrap and bake, covered, in 400°

oven for 45 minutes. Uncover and bake until bubbly hot. Remove from oven, stir in filé powder and serve at once over rice.

Serves 4 to 6.

To serve seafood gumbo: Uncover and set freezer container in a pan of cold water until sufficiently thawed to transfer to four or six individual casserole dishes. Add shrimp and oysters. Place in preheated 400° oven to bake until bubbly hot. Serve with crusty Italian or French bread.

Serves 4 to 6.

ASPARAGUS in SHERRY CREAM SAUCE (to serve now) and CHICKEN HASH St. REGIS (for the freezer)

For Asparagus in Sherry Cream Sauce

24 fresh asparagus stalks, trimmed
    Water
 4 tablespoons butter
 4 tablespoons flour
 2 cups chicken stock, heated
 ½ cup cream at room temperature
 ½ cup dry sherry
    Salt
 ½ cup slivered almonds
 ½ cup grated sharp Cheddar cheese

For Chicken Hash St. Regis

½ cup slivered almonds
½ cup grated sharp Cheddar cheese
2 cups boned and skinned, diced cooked chicken or turkey
1 cup diced cooked carrots
½ package frozen peas, sufficiently thawed to separate peas
4 tablespoons buttered bread crumbs

For asparagus in sherry cream sauce: Place the asparagus in a skillet with cold water to cover. Bring to a boil and simmer 10 to 15 minutes, or until just tender. Drain. Arrange in 4 or 6 individual shallow, oval au gratin dishes. In a saucepan melt the butter and stir in the flour. When blended add the heated stock and stir vigorously with a whisk until smooth. Stir in cream and sherry. Season with salt. Sprinkle ½ cup of almonds over the asparagus and spoon half of the sauce over, then sprinkle with ½ cup grated cheese. (Can be prepared ahead to this point. Cover sauce directly with plastic wrap to keep film from forming. Leave at room temperature for up to one-half hour, or refrigerate up to 3 hours.) Bake in preheated 400° oven until sauce is bubbly.

Serves 4 to 6.

For chicken hash St. Regis: Add ½ cup almonds and ½ cup cheese to remaining sauce. Stir until cheese is melted. Add remaining ingredients and fork-stir. Spoon into 6 individual (shallow) au gratin freezer-to-oven dishes. Cover, wrap and freeze.

To serve: Unwrap and bake in covered, preheated 400° oven for 30 minutes. Uncover and continue to bake until thoroughly heated.. Serve in baking dishes.

Serves 6.

ROLLED BREAST OF CHICKEN
with PROSCIUTTO and CHEESE

3 whole raw chicken breasts
6 thin slices prosciutto or boiled ham
6 thin slices mozzarella cheese
2 teaspoons butter
1 egg, lightly beaten
1 cup seasoned Italian bread crumbs

Cut breasts in half through the center bone. Remove skin and bones. Place between two sheets of waxed paper and pound thin. Cover each chicken piece with a slightly smaller slice of ham. Place a still smaller slice of cheese on the ham. Dot with slivers of butter. Roll jelly-roll fashion: tuck in ends of chicken pieces to roll easily and make a neat small loaf. Dip each roll in beaten egg, and roll in bread crumbs. Place on flat surface, seam side down.* Freeze until firm. Wrap separately in foil, or package in single layers in freezer container. Return to freezer.

To serve: Place, not touching, in shallow baking dish. Bake at 350° for 1 to 1½ hours.

These little rolls look as elegant as they taste and are deceptively simple to make. Serve them plain or covered with rich white sauce or with a traditional Italian sauce made with tomatoes.

Makes 6 rolls

*To serve without freezing, chill in refrigerator for 4 to 6 hours before baking at 350° for 30 minutes.

Never have I eaten a tamale pie in Mexico, but I've had it often in Texas, having lived in that state for many happy years. I say—in true Lone Star fashion—if your guests don't like this, well, they just don't know what's good.

CHICKEN TAMALE PIE

An inexpensive but different dish for a party, using leftover chicken or turkey. Easily doubled if you want to make one for now and one for the freezer.

    1   dozen canned tamales
    1   12-ounce can kernel corn
    1   cup cooked leftover diced chicken or turkey
    2   cups canned tomatoes
    4   slices crisp fried bacon
    1   teaspoon chili powder
    ¼   cup crumbled Fritos corn chips
    ¼   cup butter
    ½   teaspoon salt
    1   teaspoon Worcestershire sauce
 1½   cups chicken stock
    1   cup grated mild American cheese

Cut tamales into 2-inch pieces. Place in a well-buttered casserole. Place remaining ingredients except cheese in a large mixing bowl. Blend well and pour over tamales. Bake at 300° for 1 hour.* Remove from oven. Cool slightly, wrap and freeze.

To serve: Bake for 1 to 1½ hours at 300°. Sprinkle casserole liberally with grated cheese. Return to oven until cheese melts.

Serves 6 to 8.

*To serve without freezing, bake for 30 to 40 minutes, sprinkle with cheese, and return to oven until cheese melts.

6

From the Sea

Oysters! What wonderful morsels these are. I don't care if they are great nutrition—that's nice and I'm glad—but what I really care about is that they taste so perfectly divine. I once served scalloped deviled oysters at a buffet and dismally watched two otherwise polite people eat the whole dish down to the last oyster—it was meant to serve eight! As for the baked oysters Italian style, I just hope someday to get enough of them. You will, too.

BAKED OYSTERS ITALIAN STYLE (for now)
and
SCALLOPED DEVILED OYSTERS (for the freezer)

3 pints oysters
¼ pound butter, melted and mixed with 4 cups fresh white bread crumbs from a loaf of Italian or French bread (use your blender or tear apart and shred with a fork)

For the Scalloped Deviled Oysters

1 egg yolk
¼ teaspoon Worcestershire sauce
½ cup bottled Sauce Diable
½ teaspoon salt
¼ teaspoon pepper
½ cup oyster liquid
¾ cup milk
½ cup dry sherry

For the Baked Oysters Italian Style

2 cloves garlic, very finely minced
2 tablespoons butter, soft
¼ cup oyster liquid
¼ cup finely minced parsley
¼ cup freshly grated Parmesan cheese
½ cup minced smoked ham
¼ cup butter slivers

For the scalloped oysters: Spread a shallow freezer-to-oven baking dish with a layer of crumbs. Cover with a layer of oysters. Repeat, then cover with a layer of crumbs. In total use 1 pint oysters and about half of the buttered crumbs. Combine remaining ingredients. Blend in electric blender or in a bowl, using a whisk to blend thoroughly. Pour over oysters and crumbs. Wrap and freeze.

For the baked oysters: In a large skillet sauté the garlic in 1 tablespoon of the butter until limp. Add the remaining buttered crumbs and blend. Stir in parsley and ham. Remove from heat. Spread remaining butter on the bottom and sides of a shallow baking dish. Cover the bottom of the dish with about half of the crumbs, garlic and parsley mixture and arrange the remaining oysters over them. Stir the grated cheese with remaining crumbs and sprinkle them over the oysters. Bake in a preheated 350° oven for 10 to 15 minutes or until crumbs are browned.

Serves 4 to 6.

To bake the frozen scalloped oysters: Unwrap, bake, covered, in preheated 400° oven for 30 minutes. Uncover, pour sherry over surface, dot with slivers of butter and continue to bake 20 to 30 minutes, or until bubbly hot and top crumbs are browned.

Serves 4 to 6.

Scallops are lovely sautéed, fried or broiled, but have you ever scalloped a scallop? The results are super delicious for Sunday night supper or a festive lunch. I add a salad of cold broccoli vinaigrette and my "rajah pudding"—a layer of frozen raspberries, a layer of lemon or orange sherbet, plus a third thick layer of sour cream, sweetened with brown sugar. The whole thing is frozen in one casserole or individual ramekins and makes for a perfect ending after the creamy scallop casserole.

As for scallop salad, this is right from the sunny French Riviera, a perfect choice for a summer day's terrace lunch.

SCALLOP SALAD (for a luncheon main course now) and SCALLOPED SCALLOPS (for the freezer)

4 pounds fresh or frozen scallops
  Water

For the Salad

2 tablespoons fresh lemon juice
1 tablespoon capers, thoroughly drained
2 talbespoons minced parsley
1 cup chopped celery
2 cups mayonnaise
  Lettuce leaves
  Black olives
  Tomato wedges

For the Scalloped Scallops

½ pound fresh mushrooms, trimmed and finely chopped
¼ pound butter
2½ cups bread crumbs made from French or Italian bread, crust removed
⅓ cup grated Swiss cheese
1 cup light cream
½ cup dry white wine

Barely cover the scallops with cold water in a deep skillet and slowly bring to a boil over moderate heat. Drain. If using large sea scallops cut them in half.

For the salad: Place half of the scallops in a mixing bowl. Add the lemon juice, capers, parsley, celery and mayonnaise. Toss to blend. Cover and refrigerate until chilled. Serve on lettuce leaves and garnish with olives and tomato wedges.

For the scalloped scallops: Sauté the chopped mushrooms in the butter in a large skillet. Remove from heat and stir in the bread crumbs. Line a shallow buttered freezer-to-oven baking dish with crumb mixture. Cover with half of the scallops, repeat twice. Mix remaining crumbs with cheese and sprinkle over top layer of scallops. Combine cream and wine, and pour over surface. Cover, wrap and freeze.

To serve: Unwrap and bake, covered, in preheated 400° oven for 30 minutes. Uncover and continue to bake until thoroughly heated and topping is golden brown.

Serves 6 to 8.

Shrimp are expensive. True, but if you use them to make a true shrimp Creole to serve over lots of hot white rice and at the same time use the same sauce for a thrifty lima bean casserole, the budget is balanced and the results are delicious eating at any price.

INEXPENSIVE LIMA BEAN and MUSHROOM CASSEROLE (for tonight) and SHRIMP CREOLE (to freeze for a party)

For Creole Sauce

½ cup chopped boiled or baked ham
1 large onion, minced
¼ small green pepper, minced
2 stalks celery, minced
1 tablespoon mild vegetable oil
1 tablespoon butter
2 1-pound cans tomatoes
1 bay leaf
2 teaspoons sugar
4 to 5 dashes Tabasco sauce
¼ cup fresh lemon juice

For Lima Bean Casserole

4 cups canned lima beans, drained (or use fresh or frozen cooked limas)
1 6-ounce can sliced mushrooms, drained
¼ cup fine dry seasoned bread crumbs
2 tablespoons melted butter

For Shrimp Creole

1 pound shrimp, shelled and deveined
1 tablespoon parsley, minced
3 cups cooked white rice

For Creole sauce: Sauté the ham, onion, green pepper and celery in oil and butter until vegetables are limp. Add tomatoes, bay leaf, sugar and Tabasco sauce. Bring to a boil, lower heat and let simmer for about 15 minutes. Stir flour into lemon juice and stir this into the sauce.

For the lima bean casserole: Place the lima beans and mushrooms in a baking dish. Add half of the sauce. Fork-stir to blend. Combine bread crumbs and melted butter. Spoon over vegetables and sauce. Bake in 375° oven until thoroughly heated and topping is lightly browned.

For shrimp Creole: Add shrimp to remaining sauce and cook, stirring gently until shrimp are firm and pink. Transfer to freezer-to-oven-to-table casserole. Wrap and freeze.

To serve frozen shrimp Creole casserole: Unwrap and bake, covered, in 450° oven for 30 minutes. Uncover, stir in parsley, and bake until heated through. Serve over hot rice.

Each dish serves 4.

Broccoli Mornay sounds so extra special. It is a special dish but it's easy to make and the Mornay sauce goes on to greater glories for crab meat au gratin, a really festive luncheon main course.

BROCCOLI MORNAY (to Serve Now)
and
CRAB MEAT au GRATIN (for the Freezer)

Crab meat is such a luxury I ease my conscience by using the sauce, which must be made first, for broccoli Mornay and freeze the crab meat au gratin for a party dish.

Both dishes are very quick and easy to prepare. The broccoli Mornay can be prepared ahead and then baked after guests arrive. The crab meat au gratin need only be placed frozen in the oven to bake and serve in their same individual freezer-to-oven-to-table dishes.

For Broccoli Mornay

    1 cup lean ham cubes, left over from baked ham (optional)
    1 bunch broccoli, about 1½ pounds, or 1 10-ounce package
       frozen broccoli
    4 slices white bread, crust removed
    2 tablespoons butter
    4 tablespoons flour
 1½ cups milk, heated
    ½ cup dry sherry
    3 egg yolks, beaten
    ½ cup grated Gruyère or Swiss cheese
       Salt
       Pepper
    4 tablespoons fine dry bread crumbs

For Crab Meat au Gratin

2 cups lump crab meat
½ cup packaged chicken stuffing mix
2 tablespoons grated Parmesan cheese
Paprika

For broccoli Mornay: Bring ham to room temperature. Cook broccoli until it is just done. Drain, break up into florets. Add ham. Toast bread, cut each slice in half and place in bottom of four individual shallow baking dishes. Cover each with broccoli and ham. In a saucepan melt the butter and stir in flour. When blended add the heated milk and stir vigorously with a whisk. Stir sherry into beaten egg yolks and add to sauce, stirring rapidly with whisk. Add cheese and stir until sauce is very thick and smooth. Season with salt and pepper. Spoon about ½ cup sauce over each serving of broccoli and ham. Sprinkle each with bread crumbs. (May be made ahead to this point.) Cover sauce directly with plastic wrap to keep film from forming. Let stand at room temperature up to 30 minutes or refrigerate 1 to 2 hours before baking.) Bake in preheated 400° oven for 10 to 20 minutes or until sauce bubbles and crumbs are browned.

Serves 4.

For crab meat au gratin: Add crab meat and stuffing mix to remaining sauce. Gently fork-stir to blend. Spoon into four buttered freezer-to-oven individual au gratin dishes. Sprinkle with Parmesan cheese and paprika. Wrap and freeze. To serve: Unwrap. Bake, covered, at 400° for 30 minutes. Uncover and continue to bake until sauce bubbles. Serve from baking dishes.

Serves 4

Maryland is famous for crab meat and chicken recipes. I'm told this one is a favorite of that famous Baltimorian, the Duchess of Windsor.

MARYLAND CRAB MEAT
and CHICKEN CASSEROLE
(Some for now—some for later)

4 tablespoons butter
3 tablespoons flour
2 cups chicken broth
1 teaspoon salt
¾ teaspoon paprika
1 teaspoon pepper
⅛ teaspoon nutmeg
⅛ teaspoon garlic salt
2 cups sour cream
2 cups flaked crab meat
2 cups cooked chicken, cut in bite-sized pieces
½ cup slivered almonds
· 1 cup buttered bread crumbs

Melt butter in top half of double boiler, add flour, and stir until bubbly; add chicken broth. Cook, stirring, until thick and smooth. Add salt, paprika, pepper, nutmeg, and garlic salt. Cook 3 to 4 minutes, stirring frequently. Add sour cream; mix well. Stir in crab meat, chicken, and almonds. Pour into 6 or 8 individual freezer-to-oven-to-table casseroles. Sprinkle with bread crumbs. Bake portion to be served now in 350° oven until bubbly hot. Wrap remaining casseroles and freeze.

To serve frozen portion: Bake, covered, in 400° oven for 30 minutes. Uncover and continue to bake until heated.

Serves 6 to 8.

There's nothing more pleasant than to be able to ask a few friends to stop by for a drink and to have a really interesting substantial appetizer ready to serve in minutes. These shrimp are my never-fail standbys. Place them in the refrigerator in the morning—they will be defrosted and ready to broil by the time you are ready to put the ice in the glasses.

BROILED SHRIMP

24 jumbo shrimp
½ cup olive oil
½ cup dry sherry vinegar
2 cloves garlic, peeled
½ teaspoon salt

Shell and devein the shrimp, marinate in oil, sherry vinegar, garlic and salt overnight in the refrigerator. Remove the garlic, and freeze shrimp in the marinade. To serve: Defrost, drain and broil very close to high flame until shrimp turn a soft, rosy pink. Serve hot. Or place frozen marinade and shrimp in saucepan or chafing dish and heat. Have a platter of cocktail rye bread rounds near by, plus cocktail sauce hot with horseradish to serve as a dip.

Serves 6 to 8.

7

Appetizer and Main Course Pies

Most of us think of pies as dessert, but a flaky pie crust is even better, to my way of thinking, when made with a tomato and onion filling or as an elegant quiche lorraine. And for more substantial fare there's glazed ham pie, delicious served hot or cold.

FLAKY PLAIN PASTRY

4 cups sifted flour
2 teaspoons salt
1½ cups shortening
¾ cup ice water (approximate)

Combine flour, salt and shortening. Cut shortening into flour and salt with a pastry blender until it resembles fine cornmeal. You can do this with your fingers but a pastry blender does the job best. Quickly stir in the ice water to form pastry into a soft ball. Divide to form 4 balls. Roll each out separately on a lightly floured canvas pastry cloth, one at a time, and line a 9″ pie tin with each portion. Handle pastry as little as possible and fill tins loosely (no stretching). Wrap tightly in aluminum foil, seal and freeze until needed.

Makes 4 pie crust shells.

SALMON QUICHE

1 frozen pie shell
2 tablespoons butter
2 tablespoons finely minced shallots
1 10-ounce package frozen chopped spinach
1 8-ounce can red salmon
¼ teaspoon freshly ground black pepper
4 eggs, lightly beaten

Bake frozen pie shell in preheated 400° oven until very lightly browned, about 10 minutes. Remove from oven and lower heat to 375°. Melt the butter in a large skillet, add the shallots and sauté until limp. Add the frozen block of spinach and the liquid from salmon. Cover and cook over low heat until frozen block of spinach is thawed and can be separated. Turn several times as it cooks and break up with a fork. Add salmon and flake with a fork. Cook, stirring 2 or 3 minutes. Add hot scalded milk to egg, beating with whisk. Add spinach and salmon mixture, blend and pour into pie shell. Bake at 375° for 30 minutes or until set.

Serves 4 to 6 as a main course.

Serves 6 to 8 as a first-course appetizer.

ITALIAN QUICHE with SAUSAGE

1 frozen pie shell
½ pound bulk sausage meat
1 large tomato, skinned, seeded and chopped
½ teaspoon salt
¼ teaspoon freshly ground black pepper
½ teaspoon mixed Italian herbs
1½ cups cream
4 eggs lightly beaten
1 tablespoon tomato paste

Place frozen pie shell in preheated 450° oven and bake until very lightly browned, about 15 minutes. Remove and reduce oven to 375°. In a large skillet cook sausage meat until browned, pour off all rendered fat. Add tomato, salt, pepper and herbs and cook for 2 or 3 minutes. Scald the cream, add to the eggs while beating with a whisk. Add tomato paste and beat until blended. Stir in sausage-tomato mixture and pour all into pie shell. Bake for about 30 minutes or until custard has set.

Serves 4 to 6.

TOMATO ONION PIE

1 frozen pie shell
1 large purple onion
½ cup milk
2 large firm tomatoes
½ teaspoon salt
½ teaspoon pepper
½ teaspoon mixed Italian herbs
1 tablespoon butter
1 tablespoon chopped parsley

Place pie shell in 450° oven and bake for 8 to 10 minutes. Remove from oven and set aside. Reduce oven heat to 350°. Peel onion and cut into very thin slices, break into rings. Place in a shallow nonmetal dish and cover with milk. Allow onions to soak for at least 30 minutes. Peel tomatoes by plunging them into boiling water for a moment and then slipping the skins off with the point of a small knife. Cut tomatoes into fairly thick slices. Arrange on the bottom of the pie shell. Drain onions well and arrange rings on top of tomatoes. Sprinkle with salt, pepper and Italian herbs. Place in 350° oven and bake 15 to 20 minutes or until tomatoes are soft but still firm. Sprinkle with parsley and serve hot as a first course or as a luncheon dish. Serves 6.

QUICK MAIN DISH QUICHE with HAM

1 frozen pie shell
1 cup light cream
3 eggs

½ teaspoon salt
½ teaspoon black pepper
1 cup chopped ham
½ cup grated Swiss cheese
¼ cup chopped parsley

Place frozen pie shell in preheated 450° oven and bake for 8 to 10 minutes. Remove pie shell from oven and lower heat to 350°. Place cream in a saucepan and heat to just luke warm (do not allow to boil). Beat eggs until frothy, add salt, pepper and cream. Blend well. Spread chopped ham and cheese over bottom of pie shell, pour in egg mixture. Place in oven and bake for 25 to 30 minutes or until custard is set. Sprinkle with parsley just before serving.

Serves 6.

GLAZED HAM PIE

1 frozen pie shell
1 pound ground ham (leftover ham from the freezer is perfect)
1 cup milk
1½ cups fine dry bread crumbs
½ teaspoon pepper

For Glaze

½ cup brown sugar
3 tablespoons vinegar
2 tablespoons water
¼ teaspoon dry mustard

Bake frozen pie shell in preheated 450° oven for 8 to 10

minutes. Remove and set aside. Lower oven heat to 350°. Combine ham, milk, bread crumbs and pepper. Blend well, let stand for about 30 minutes. Pile mixture into pie shell, cover with aluminum foil and bake for 20 minutes. While pie is baking, place brown sugar, vinegar, water and dry mustard in a small saucepan and bring to a boil, stirring constantly. Lower heat and continue to cook until sugar has dissolved. Uncover ham pie and pour glaze over surface. Return pie to oven and bake uncovered for a final 10 minutes. Serve hot or cold.

Serves 6.

8

Crêpes and their Fillings

What is the mystique about crêpes? The truth is that crêpes are easy to make, in fact, fun. Once you get the knack of them, the temptation is to just stand there making crêpe after crêpe. More important, there is nothing nicer to have in your freezer. Crêpes filled with a creamed seafood or chicken filling will serve as a luncheon or supper main course, or, if you want to be extravagant on some special occasion, try them with a filling of red caviar, topped with a spoonful of sour cream.

As for dessert, crêpes are the easy out for lazy cooks who want perfect endings; filled with any number of fruit fillings or ice cream plus a quick-to-make sauce or splash of liqueur, they live up to their reputation as the "gourmet's dessert."

CRÊPES

¾ cup milk
¼ cup cognac or orange liqueur
3 eggs
1 cup flour
¼ teaspoon salt
1 tablespoon sugar
5 tablespoons butter, melted
  Butter for frying

Place ingredients in order listed in container of electric blender and blend at high speed for about 10 seconds, then turn off the machine and with a rubber spatula or wooden spoon scrape down the flour patches which will have collected on the sides of the container. Blend at high speed again, this time for about a minute or until smooth. Refrigerate 2 hours or as long as you like. Stir batter well before using. For each crêpe heat about ½ teaspoon butter in a 7- or 8-inch crêpe pan over medium-high heat. Pour in scant ¼ cup batter quickly, tilting pan to distribute batter evenly. When light brown, turn and lightly brown other side. Slip onto paper toweling.

To freeze: Separate crêpes in stacks with waxed paper, wrap airtight in heavy foil or freezer paper. Will keep about 3 months. Crêpes thaw quickly at room temperature.

Makes about 12 crêpes.

APPETIZER CRÊPES with
HAM and CHEESE FILLING

12 crêpes, freshly made or frozen and thawed
 1 4-ounce jar Smithfield ham spread
 4 slices Cheddar cheese

Spread each crêpe with Smithfield ham spread. Stack slices of cheese and cut stacks across, making twelve "finger" strips. Place one strip on each crêpe, roll up, and fold ends under. Place seam side down on a lightly buttered baking sheet. Freeze until firm. Pack in plastic bags. Seal bag and store crêpes in freezer until ready to bake.

To serve place frozen filled crêpes on an ungreased baking sheet. Bake in preheated 400° oven until filling is soft (about 15 minutes).

Makes about 12 crêpes.

CRÊPES with CURRIED SHRIMP

12 frozen crêpes
 4 tablespoons butter
 1 small tart apple, peeled, cored, seeded, and very finely minced
 1 small white onion, very finely minced
 1 tablespoon curry powder
 3 tablespoons flour
 1½ cups chicken stock, combined with ½ cup milk and heated to boiling point
 1 egg yolk
 1 pound cooked shrimp, shelled, deveined and chopped
   Salt
   Pepper
 1 tablespoon grated Parmesan cheese
 1 tablespoon fine dry bread crumbs

Unwrap frozen crêpes. Thaw at room temperature while preparing filling. Melt butter in a saucepan over low heat, add apple and onion and cook, stirring frequently until reduced to a puree (at least 15 minutes). Stir in curry powder and cook, stirring, about 10 seconds. Add flour, blend, then add hot stock-and-milk mixture. Stir rapidly with a whisk until smooth and thick. Remove from heat, cool slightly, add egg yolk and stir rapidly with whisk until blended. Add shrimp and season to taste with salt and pepper. Put a spoonful of mixture on each thawed crêpe and roll up, folding in the side and arranging in a single layer in a long shallow freezer-to-oven-to-table baking dish. Spoon remaining mixture over the top. Cover, wrap and freeze.

To serve: Unwrap and bake covered in a preheated 400° oven for 45 minutes. Uncover, sprinkle with grated cheese and bread crumbs and continue to bake until bubbly hot. Serve from the dish.

Serves 4.

CRÊPES MONSIEUR

12 frozen crêpes
12 thin slices lean baked ham, each a little smaller than crêpes
12 thin slices Swiss cheese, each a little smaller than the ham
   slices

Cheese Sauce

1 ¼ cup grated Cheddar cheese
1 teaspoon butter
¼ cup stale beer
   Salt
   Pepper

For crêpes monsieur: Thaw crepes at room temperature. Cover each with a slice of ham and one of cheese. Roll up and place seam side down, side by side, in a shallow baking dish just large enough to hold them compactly. Bake in preheated 375° oven for 10 minutes. Arrange on warm serving plates and spoon cheese sauce over each serving. Serve at once.

For cheese sauce: Combine all ingredients in top of double boiler. Stir over simmering water until heated and smooth. Makes about 1 ¼ cups sauce.

Serves 4 to 6 as an appetizer or first course, 3 or 4 as a luncheon dish.

CRÊPES with DIVINE SHRIMP

1 cup clam juice
1 pound fresh shrimp
3 tablespoons butter
3 tablespoons flour
1 cup milk
¼ cup dry white wine
1 tablespoon dry sherry
1 tablespoon minced chives
　Salt
　Pepper
12 crêpes from the freezer

Heat clam juice to boiling. Add shrimp and cook until firm and pink (about 3 minutes). Drain, reserving clam juice. Shell, devein and coarsely chop shrimp. Melt butter in a saucepan and stir in flour. Slowly add reserved clam juice, stirring as added. Add milk, wine and sherry. Stir until sauce thickens. Add chives and shrimp. Taste and add salt if needed (clam juice is salty). Thaw and heat crêpes in a 350° oven. Place on heated serving plates. Spoon some of the shrimp and sauce on one side of each. Fold crêpe over filling, spoon additional sauce over surface and serve at once.

Serves 4.

Crêpes Suzette are customarily made at the table in full view of the appreciative diners. The crêpes themselves can be from the freezer, but the cooked crêpes and the ingredients for the sauce are brought into the dining room for the final flourishes.

CRÊPES SUZETTE

4 lumps sugar
1 orange
1 teaspoon lemon juice
1 tablespoon butter
2 tablespoons Curaçao
2 tablespoons Grand Marnier
¼ cup cognac, warmed in a small saucepan before use

Thaw 12 frozen crêpes and bring them to the table on a heated serving dish.

Rub the lumps of sugar against the orange rind and crush them in the top pan of the chafing dish over direct heat. Cut orange in half and extract juice. Add orange juice, lemon juice and butter and stir well. Pour in the Curaçao and Grand Marnier, and bring the sauce to a boil. Put the crêpes in the sauce one by one, turning them to saturate them in the sauce. Fold each crêpe and put it to one side of the pan. When all the crêpes are sauced and folded, sprinkle them with the warmed cognac. Set the cognac ablaze and baste the crêpes until the flame dies out. Serve at once.

Serves 6.

FRUIT-FILLED CRÊPES

2 cups peeled and sliced strawberries or peaches
2 tablespoons orange juice
3 tablespoons sugar
1 tablespoon tapioca
1 tablespoon Kirsch or Grand Marnier liqueur
   Powdered sugar
12 crêpes (from freezer)

Combine fruit, orange juice and sugar in a small saucepan.
Cook over low heat just until fruit begins to soften and sugar has
dissolved. Stir in tapioca and liqueur and cook, stirring over
low heat until mixture has thickened. Cool slightly. Arrange
crêpes in shallow oven-to-table casserole. Spoon filling onto
one side of each crêpe, fold over and dust with powdered sugar.
Place in preheated 350° oven for 10 to 15 minutes until filling is
bubbly hot. Serve at once.
Serves 6

CRÊPES ALASKA

This is not an authentic Alaska but it tastes so superb it's not a
bad idea to double the recipe—almost everyone at my house
asks for second helpings.

1½ cups bottled caramel sauce
⅓ cup light rum
12 crêpes (from freezer)
    French vanilla ice cream from the freezer (about 1½ pints)

Put sauce and rum in the top of a double boiler over simmering water until heated. Then heat crêpes in 350° oven. Place two on each dessert plate. Put a small scoop of ice crean on one side of each crêpe and fold over. Spoon hot sauce on top and serve at once.
Serves 6.

CRÊPES CUBANAISE

12 crêpes (from freezer)
1 8-ounce can crushed pineapple, well drained
¼ cup apricot jam
Confectioners' sugar
¼ cup light rum

Thaw crêpes at room temperature about 15 minutes. Combine well-drained pineapple and jam in top of double boiler over simmering water. Stir until heated. Put a spoonful of the pineapple mixture on each crêpe and roll up. Place them seam side down and side by side in a shallow baking dish just large enough to hold them. Sprinkle generously with powdered sugar. Put in preheated 375° oven for about 5 minutes. Then place under broiler heat until sugar is lightly browned. Heat the rum in a small skillet. Ignite and pour over crêpes. Bring to the table and serve as soon as flame subsides.
Serves 4 to 6.

APRICOT CRÊPES with ICE CREAM

6 tablespoons apricot jam
1 tablespoon cognac or orange liqueur

6 crêpes
1 tablespoon sugar
1 tablespoon butter
  French vanilla ice cream

Combine apricot jam and cognac or orange liqueur. Spread each crêpe with some of the mixture and roll up. Place rolled crêpes, side by side, in a shallow, well-buttered baking dish that is just large enough to hold them compactly. Sprinkle with sugar and dot with butter. Wrap well in heavy-duty foil. Label, date and freeze.

To serve: Remove freezer wrap. Cover dish with regular foil. Bake in a 450° oven for 10 minutes. Uncover and continue to bake until crêpes are thoroughly heated. Place a small scoop of French vanilla ice cream on each portion.

Serves 3 or 4.

9

A Few Quick Ones from the Freezer

All manner of frozen fish and shellfish lie ready in your supermarket—usually a bargain, too. And you can make economical use of extra chicken pieces not needed for a particular dish by freezing them to have ready to transform into elegant, different main courses. The trick is to give these handy foods some interesting flavor—try sweet and sour shrimp or shrimp or chicken Hawaiian or easy Italian-flavored fish fillets. In any event, you get my point. With a few interesting recipes and a small supply of frozen fish or chicken in your freezer you'll have the makings of really good main dishes to get to the table quickly and easily.

BAKED FISH STEAKS
BASQUE STYLE

4 frozen fish steak portions (cod, halibut, swordfish)
2 tablespoons olive oil
1 medium-sized onion, chopped
2 cloves garlic, minced
½ small green pepper, chopped
1 tablespoon flour
1 1-pound can stewed tomatoes
6 or 8 pimento-stuffed green olives, sliced
  Salt
  Pepper

Arrange frozen fish steaks in a shallow oiled baking dish. Heat the oil in a small skillet. In it sauté the onion, garlic and green pepper until vegetables are limp. Stir in flour. Add tomatoes and cook, stirring often, for about 10 minutes. Stir in olives and season with salt and pepper. Pour over fish. Cover and bake in preheated 350° oven for 25 minutes. Uncover and continue to bake until fish flakes easily when touched with a fork (about 15 minutes).

Serves 4.

SHRIMP FLORENTINE

2 10-ounce packages frozen chopped spinach
4 tablespoons butter at room temperature
  Water
½ cup dry white wine or vermouth
3 or 4 peppercorns

1 10-ounce package frozen cleaned and deveined shrimp
1 egg yolk, beaten
½ cup milk
2 tablespoons grated Parmesan cheese

Cook spinach according to package directions. Drain, reserving the water. Stir 2 tablespoons of the butter into the spinach and spread it out on the bottom of a long, shallow baking dish. Add sufficient water to the spinach water to total ¾ cup and combine it in the spinach saucepan with the wine. Add the peppercorns, bring to a boil, lower heat and let simmer for about 10 minutes. Bring again to a boil and add frozen shrimp. Let cook until shrimp are firm and pink. Remove from heat, remove and discard peppercorns, remove shrimp with a slotted spoon to a chopping board and coarse chop. Sprinkle over spinach. Melt the remaining 2 tablespoons of butter in a second saucepan and stir in the flour. Bring the liquid in which the shrimp were cooked to a boil and add to the butter–flour mixture, stirring rapidly with a whisk. Continue to whisk-stir until sauce is smooth. Mix beaten egg with milk and stir this into the sauce. Cook, stirring until thickened. Pour sauce over shrimp and spinach. Sprinkle with cheese and bake in preheated 400° oven for 10 minutes. Serve from the dish.

Serves 4 to 6.

SWEET and SOUR SHRIMP

1 1-pound package frozen cooked, cleaned and deveined shrimp
2 medium-sized carrots, scraped and cut, Chinese fashion, at a 45° angle into thin oval slices.
1 green pepper, seeded and cut into bite-size cubes
1½ cups chicken stock
2 tablespoons white vinegar

2 tablespoons sugar
1 8-ounce can unsweetened pineapple chunks
2 small tomatoes, cut into wedges
1 tablespoon cornstarch
2 tablespoons soy sauce
3 cups cooked white rice

Let frozen shrimp stand at room temperature while preparing sauce. Put sliced carrots and green pepper in a small skillet and cover with water. Bring to a boil and boil until barely tender, drain and set aside. Combine stock, vinegar, sugar and juice from pineapple in a saucepan. Bring to a boil and then lower heat to simmer. Add carrots, green pepper, tomatoes and shrimp. Cook, stirring, until shrimp are heated and liquid returns to simmering. Combine cornstarch with soy sauce and stir into liquid. Simmer until sauce is thickened. Serve with rice.

Serves 4.

SHRIMP HAWAIIAN

1 tablespoon mild oil
2 or 3 drops sesame oil (optional)
½ cup chopped onion
½ cup chopped green pepper
½ cup diagonally sliced celery
½ cup chopped water chestnuts
1 14½-ounce can tomatoes
1 8-ounce can unsweetened pineapple chunks
¼ teaspoon garlic salt
¼ teaspoon pepper
1 pound frozen boiled shrimp, shelled and deveined
2 tablespoons cornstarch
Cooked white rice

Heat oil in a heavy skillet. In it stir-fry onion, green pepper and celery for about 2 or 3 minutes. Add water chestnuts and tomatoes. Drain and add pineapple, reserving juice. Season with salt and pepper. Cover and simmer for 5 minutes. Add shrimp and stir-fry until thawed and hot. Mix reserved pineapple juice with cornstarch. Stir into shrimp-vegetable mixture. Cook, stirring until sauce thickens. Serve over rice.

Serves 4.

FISH FILLETS in FOIL

1 pound frozen fish fillets
4 tablespoons butter, melted
2 tablespoons lemon juice
¼ teaspoon salt
¼ teaspoon mixed Italian herbs or basil (optional)
¼ teaspoon paprika

Cut the frozen block of fish into four equal pieces. Put each piece separately on a length of well-buttered heavy-duty foil or a double thickness of regular foil. Pour 1 tablespoon butter and ½ tablespoon lemon juice over each. Turn the fish so that both sides are coated with butter and lemon juice. Sprinkle with salt and, if desired, mixed Italian herbs or basil, and paprika. Make a "drug store" wrap of foil around each piece of fish by bringing the opposite sides of foil together evenly, then folding down in a series of folds but leaving some space between the fish and top of foil. Fold the ends toward the center. Put the foil-wrapped fish into a shallow baking dish or on a baking sheet. Bake in 450° oven for 30 minutes.

Serves 4.

FISH FILLETS in WHITE WINE SAUCE

1   pound frozen fish fillets (any kind)
¼   cup flour
½   teaspoon seasoned salt
⅛   teaspoon pepper
4   tablespoons butter
½   pound fresh mushrooms, trimmed and sliced
2   tablespoons minced chives, fresh or frozen
½   cup milk
½   cup dry white wine
    Paprika

Cut the frozen fish fillets crosswise into 8 equal pieces. Mix the flour, seasoned salt and pepper on a sheet of foil and roll fish pieces in it until evenly coated. (Reserve leftover flour.) Place flour-coated fish in a lightly buttered baking dish. Melt 2 tablespoons of the butter in a saucepan. In it sauté the mushrooms and chives for 3 to 4 minutes. Remove them with a slotted spoon and scatter them over the fish. Add the remaining butter to the saucepan. When melted, stir in the reserved flour and blend well. Slowly add the milk and wine. Stir until smooth. Pour mixture over fish and mushrooms. Cover the dish and seal with foil or with a tight fitting lid. Bake in preheated 450° oven for 25 minutes. Sprinkle with paprika just before serving.

Serves 4.

SWEET and SOUR CHICKEN

8 frozen chicken legs or thighs (or other parts)
1 tablespoon butter
1 tablespoon flour
¾ cup boiling chicken stock
1 1-pound can tomatoes
1 tablespoon brown sugar
1 tablespoon lemon juice
2 teaspoons Worcestershire sauce
½ teaspoon salt

Arrange frozen chicken pieces in a single layer, skin side up, in a shallow baking dish. Place in oven and bake at 350° until thawed (about 30 minutes). In a saucepan melt butter and stir in flour. When blended add chicken stock and stir rapidly with a whisk. Add remaining ingredients. Blend and pour over chicken pieces. Cover and bake for about 45 minutes or until chicken is very tender.

Serves 4.

HAWAIIAN BAKED CHICKEN with RICE

4 frozen chicken legs
4 frozen chicken thighs
  Salt
1 small fresh pineapple, peeled, sliced and cut into
  bite-sized cubes
½ cup chopped dates
2 tablespoons pickle juice from sweet mixed pickles
2 cups cooked long grain white rice
½ cup slivered almonds

Place frozen chicken pieces, skin side up, not touching, in a single layer in a large, shallow casserole. Place in cold oven. Set temperature at 450°. Bake for 30 minutes. Reduce temperature to 350° and continue to bake for about 15 minutes or until skin is lightly browned and crisp. Turn each piece skin side down and bake 10 minutes. Remove baking dish from heat. Remove chicken pieces. Pour all fat from pan, then return chicken pieces to it, sprinkle with salt, add pineapple and dates and return dish to oven. Bake 20 to 30 minutes or until chicken pieces are very tender. Add pickle juice, rice and almonds to dish, fork-stir and continue to bake until rice is heated. Serve from the dish.

Serves 6 to 8.

10

Take Stock in your Freezer

What does stock have to do with a freezer-to-oven-to-table cookbook? Everything. Because stock, whether chicken or beef, is sneaky freezer cooking at its best. You will not only have superb frozen nutritious stock to use in all manner of dishes, but a quick-to-prepare main dish that may be frozen or served at once. Moreover, once you try cooking with stock you will never give up the deep down satisfying taste that real homemade stock gives to soups, casseroles and creamed dishes whether frozen or not.

Stock only sounds complicated and time-consuming. It is really as easy as boiling water; any novice cook can do it. Although it has to be simmered for hours, you do not have to remain in a hot kitchen to simmer along with it. In fact, you can leave, play golf, go shopping, or simply plug away at other chores; stock will do nicely without you. You can even let it cook overnight if that's more convenient for you.

Preparing the ingredients for a stockpot requires no more than 10 to 15 minutes. Straining stock once it has been cooked and storing it in your freezer takes no more than another 10 to 15 minutes, and this includes washing. Sufficient stock can be made to last a week or a month, and as long as you have it on hand, your daily cooking chores will be so greatly lessened you'll wonder how you ever managed without it. As Escoffier said, "If one's stock is good, what remains of the cooking is easy."

CHICKEN STOCK
and
CURRIED CREAMED CHICKEN
for crêpe filling or to serve in patty shells

Chicken Stock

1 3½-to 4-pound whole chicken
1 pound chicken necks and wings
   Water
1 large white onion, peeled and quartered
1 large carrot, scraped and cut into thick slices
½ cup celery tops
¼ cup chopped parsley
1 bay leaf
4 to 6 allspice berries
2 teaspoons salt
¼ teaspoon freshly ground black pepper
1 cup dry white wine

Place whole chicken and chicken necks and wings in a large (8- to 10-quart) soup pot. Add water to cover, and bring to a boil. Lower heat, and skim surface until clear. Add remaining ingredients plus sufficient water to come to about 2 inches of rim of pot. Cover partially with a loose-fitting lid. Let simmer until whole chicken is tender, about 1½ hours. Remove chicken and let cool sufficiently to handle. Remove skin and bones from meat. Dice meat, place in a covered bowl and refrigerate. Discard skin. Return bones to stockpot. Continue to cook stock with bones for 2½ to 3 hours, or add sufficient water to come to about 2 inches of rim of pot, and let simmer very slowly overnight. Cool to room temperature. When cool, strain into containers, and refrigerate 6 hours, or overnight. Then remove from refrigerator, and discard all the fat congealed on the surface. Reserve 1 cup of stock for curried creamed chicken, pour remaining stock into 1-cup containers (those plastic containers that cottage cheese and sour cream come in are perfect), cover tightly and freeze.

Curried Creamed Chicken

2 tablespoons butter
2 tablespoons flour
1 cup clear fat-free chicken stock
½ cup milk
½ teaspoon salt
½ teaspoon pepper
1½ teaspoons Madras curry powder
1 egg yolk, lightly beaten
2 cups (approximate) diced boiled chicken
¼ cup slivered blanched almonds (optional)
¼ cup sour cream

Melt the butter in a deep heavy skillet over low heat, stir in flour and continue to cook, stirring for 3 to 4 minutes. Slowly add chicken stock, stirring constantly to blend. Add milk, salt, pepper and curry powder and continue to cook, stirring until sauce is smooth and begins to thicken. Stir a little of the hot sauce into the beaten egg yolk and add mixture to the sauce, stirring to blend until sauce is creamy thick. Add chicken. Blend and cook until chicken is thoroughly heated. If creamed chicken is to be served at once have ready six crêpes or eight patty shells (from the freezer). If the filling is to be used for crêpes (see p. 143 for crêpe recipe), place crêpes in a long shallow oven-to-table dish. Spoon filling onto one side of each crêpe, fold over and bake in a preheated 400° oven for 10 to 15 minutes until bubbly hot. If patty shells are to be used bake shells according to package directions in the same type shallow oven-to-table dish. Heat creamed chicken to serving point, spoon over just-baked shells and serve.

Sprinkle either dish with almonds and serve with sour cream.

Serves 6 to 8.

If creamed chicken is to be frozen, pour into ovenproof casserole, wrap and freeze. When ready to serve, heat in preheated 400° oven until bubbly hot and proceed as directed above.

BEEF STOCK
and
COLD SLICED BEEF in WINE JELLY

Beef Stock

2 pounds Oxtails with bone
1 veal knuckle bone (optional)
2 cups dry red wine
1 3-pound brisket of beef
1 large onion, peeled and quartered
2 medium carrots, scraped and cut into quarters
½ cup chopped celery tops
¼ cup chopped parsley
2 teaspoons salt
6 to 8 peppercorns
1 bay leaf

Put oxtails, veal knuckle bone and brisket of beef in a large roasting pan. Place in a preheated 450° oven for 30 to 45 minutes or until bones and meat are browned. Turn them occasionally so that they brown evenly on all sides. Remove pan from oven, and transfer meat and bones to a large (8- to 10-quart) soup pot. Pour 1 cup of the wine into the roasting pan, and scrape all the brown bits and pieces of meat that have clung to the pan into it. Add this to the soup pot, then add the second cup of wine, the remaining ingredients, and sufficient water to come to about 2 inches of rim of pot. Bring to a full boil. Turn heat to very low, partially cover pot with a loosely fitting lid, and let simmer for about 2 hours. Remove brisket of beef to a large platter. Cool, then cover and refrigerate. Add additional water to pot to again come to 2 inches of rim, and continue to cook stock over low heat for at least 3 hours, or let simmer very slowly overnight. Turn off heat, and cool. When cool, strain into containers, and refrigerate 6 hours or overnight. Remove from refrigerator, and discard all fat that has congealed on the surface. Reserve 1½ cups stock (for sliced beef), pour remainder of stock into 1-cup containers (cottage cheese containers are ideal). Cover tightly and freeze.

Slice meat into even ¼-inch slices, place in ovenproof casserole and cover with stock. If desired, wrap and freeze.

Cold Sliced Beef

Remove meat from freezer, place in preheated 350° oven for about 30 minutes or until thawed and stock is liquid.

For Jelly

1½ cups liquid stock
 1 envelope unflavored gelatin
 ½ cup dry red wine

½ teaspoon salt
½ teaspoon pepper
¼ teaspoon garlic salt

Garnish

Ripe olives
Tomato wedges

Heat stock in small saucepan to boiling, sprinkle gelatin over hot stock, remove from heat and stir until gelatin has dissolved. Add wine and seasonings. Stir to blend. Lightly grease a serving casserole and arrange meat slices in it. Pour stock-wine mixture over meat. Refrigerate until firm. Turn out onto a chilled platter and decorate with ripe olives and tomato wedges. This is a super buffet party dish for any warm night. Serve with homemade potato salad, crusty buttered rolls and red wine. Wind up the festivities with sliced fresh fruit, sprinkled with powdered sugar and kirsch.

Note: The beef may also be served hot—just omit the gelatin from the sauce and serve over beef with freshly boiled new potatoes and carrots. French bread, of course, to mop up the sauce. Apple Betty would be a perfect dessert for this cold-weather menu.

11

For the Bread Box

Homemade breads and rolls are so superior to the commercial variety there is simply no comparing the two, but let's face it, bread making is quite a project and most people are not in the mood to make bread every day. When you are in the mood, it's actually fun and truly soul-satisfying work, to say the least. So why not make and freeze? That way you'll have marvelous homemade bread and rolls on hand anytime you want them and the fragrance of fresh baked bread will fill your house.

CURRANT JELLY BUNS
and
FREEZER BRAIDED NUT ROLL

Dough

5½ to 6½ cups unsifted flour
  ¼ cup sugar
  1 teaspoon salt
  2 packages active dry yeast
  ½ cup (1 stick) softened butter
  1 cup very warm tap water (120°-130°)
  3 eggs (at room temperature)

Pecan Filling

  1 cup ground pecans
  3 tablespoons sugar
4½ tablespoons melted butter

For Currant Jelly Buns

Currant jelly

For Braided Nut Roll

Confectioners' sugar or confectioners' sugar frosting

Blend together ground pecans, sugar and melted butter. Refrigerate until ready to use.

For currant jelly buns: In a large bowl thoroughly mix 1¼ cups flour, sugar, salt and undissolved active dry yeast. Add butter. Gradually add tap water to dry ingredients and beat 2 minutes at medium speed of electric mixer, scraping bowl occasionally. Add eggs and ¼ cup flour. Beat at high speed 2 minutes, scraping bowl occasionally. Stir in enough additional flour to make a soft dough. Turn out onto lightly floured board; knead until smooth and elastic (about 8 to 10 minutes). Divide dough in half. Roll out one-half and cut into 1-inch strips. Twist each strip and coil into a circle, sealing ends underneath. Place on ungreased baking sheet. Make wide indentations in center of coil. Spoon currant jelly into indentations. Let rise in place, free from drafts, until double in bulk, about 45 minutes. Bake in preheated 375° oven for 15 to 20 minutes or until done. Remove from baking sheet and cool on wire rack.

For braided nut roll: Divide remaining one-half of dough into three equal pieces. Roll each piece into a 9x15-inch rectangle. Cut each into three lengthwise strips, 3x15 inches each. Spread centers of strips with ⅓ prepared pecan filling. Seal edges and ends very firmly, forming long filled ropes. Braid each three-rope section together, forming three braided ropes. Pinch ends to seal; tuck underneath. Place on greased baking sheet. Cover tightly with plastic wrap; place in freezer. When firm, remove from baking sheets and wrap each braid with plastic wrap, then with aluminum foil. Keep frozen up to four weeks.

To bake: Remove one or more ropes as desired from freezer, unwrap and place on ungreased baking sheets. Let stand, covered loosely with plastic wrap, at room temperature until fully thawed, about 2 hours. Let rise in warm place, free from draft, until more than doubled in bulk (about 2½ hours). Bake at 375° for 15 to 20 minutes or until done. Remove from baking

sheets and cool on wire racks. Sprinkle with confectioners'
sugar or frost with confectioners' sugar frosting.

CHEESY BREAD STICKS
and
FREEZER SESAME SEED BREAD STICKS

Dough

```
3  to 3½ cups unsifted flour
¼  teaspoon sugar
1½  teaspoons salt
2  packages active dry yeast
1  tablespoon softened butter
1¼  cups very warm tap water (120°-130°)
```

For Cheesy Bread Sticks

```
½  cup grated Parmesan cheese
```

For Sesame Seed Bread Sticks

```
1  egg white, beaten
1  tablespoon cold water
   Toasted sesame seed or poppy seed
```

In a large bowl thoroughly mix 1 cup flour, sugar, salt, and
undissolved active dry yeast. Add butter. Gradually add tap
water to dry ingredients and beat 2 minutes at medium speed

of electric mixer, scraping bowl occasionally. Add ½ cup flour. Beat at high speed 2 minutes, scraping bowl occasionally. Divide dough in half.

For cheesy bread sticks: Add Parmesan cheese to one half of the dough and enough additional flour to make a soft dough. Turn out onto well-floured board. Divide dough into 8 equal parts. Roll each piece of dough into a rope, 18 inches long.

Cut each rope into three 6-inch ropes. Place on ungreased baking sheet. Let rise in a warm place, free from drafts, until double in bulk. Bake in preheated 375° oven 20 to 25 minutes or until done. Remove from baking sheet and cool on wire rack.

For sesame seed bread sticks: Add sufficient flour to remaining dough to again make a soft dough. Turn out onto well-floured board. Divide into 8 equal pieces. Roll each piece of dough into a rope 18 inches long. Cut each rope into three 6-inch ropes. Place on greased baking sheets, rolling to grease all sides of dough. Cover with plastic wrap. Freeze until firm. Transfer to plastic bags. May be kept frozen up to 4 weeks.

To serve: Remove from freezer and place on ungreased baking sheets. Cover; let stand at room temperature until fully thawed (about 30 minutes). Let rise in warm place, free from draft, until doubled in bulk, about 15 minutes. Brush with combined egg white and cold water; sprinkle with seeds. Bake at 375° for 20 to 25 minutes or until done. Remove from baking sheets and cool on wire racks.

Makes a total of 4 dozen bread sticks.

FREEZER WHITE BREAD
and
CINNAMON RAISIN BREAD

Basic Dough

12½ to 13½ cups unsifted flour
 ½ cup sugar
 2 tablespoons salt
 ⅔ cup instant nonfat dry milk solids
 4 packages active dry yeast
 ¼ cup (½ stick) softened butter
 4 cups very warm tap water (120°-130°)

For Cinnamon Raisin Bread

1 cup raisins
1 tablespoon cinnamon

In a large bowl thoroughly mix 4 cups flour, sugar, salt, dry milk solids, and undissolved active dry yeast. Add butter. Gradually add tap water to dry indredients and beat 2 minutes at medium speed of electric mixer, scraping bowl occasionally. Add 1½ cups flour. Beat at high speed 2 minutes, scraping bowl occasionally. Divide dough in half.

For white bread: To one half stir in enough additional flour to form a stiff dough. Turn out on a lightly floured board, knead until smooth and elastic. Cover with a towel and let rest 15 minutes. Divide this dough into two equal parts. Form each into a smooth, round ball. Flatten each into a mound 6 inches in diameter. Place on a greased baking sheet. Cover with plastic wrap. Freeze until firm. Transfer to plastic bags. Freeze up to four weeks.

For cinnamon raisin bread: To remaining dough add raisins and cinnamon, then sufficient flour to make a stiff dough. Turn out onto lightly floured board and knead until smooth and elastic. Cover with a towel and let rest 15 minutes. Divide this dough into two equal parts. Form each into a smooth round ball. Let rise on ungreased baking sheet until doubled, about 1 hour. Bake in a preheated 350° oven about 35 minutes. Cool on wire rack.

To bake frozen loaves: Remove from freezer and place on an ungreased baking sheet. Cover and let stand at room temperature until fully thawed (about four hours). Roll each ball to 12 x 8 inches. Shape into loaves. Place in greased 8½ x 4½ x 2½-inch loaf pans. Let rise in a warm place, free from drafts, until double in bulk (about 1½ hours). Bake in preheated 350° oven for about 35 minutes or until done. Remove from pans and let cool on wire rack.

Makes 2 loaves white bread, 2 loaves cinnamon raisin bread.

FROZEN DINNER ROLLS
and
ORANGE SUGAR BUNS

Basic Dough

5½ to 6½ cups unsifted flour
 ½ cup sugar
1½ teaspoons salt

2 packages active dry yeast
1¼ cups water
½ cup milk
1 stick butter
2 eggs (at room temperature)

For Orange Sugar Buns

1 cup melted butter
1 cup sugar
¼ cup grated orange peel

In a large bowl thoroughly mix 2 cups flour, sugar, salt and undissolved active dry yeast. Combine water, milk and butter in a saucepan. Heat over low heat until liquids are very warm (120°-130°). Gradually add to dry ingredients and beat 2 minutes at medium speed of electric mixer, scraping bowl occasionally. Add eggs and ½ cup flour. Beat at high speed 2 minutes, scraping bowl occasionally. Stir in enough additional flour to make a soft dough. Turn out onto lightly floured board; knead until smooth and elastic (about 8 to 10 minutes). Cover with plastic wrap, then a towel, let rest 20 minutes. Punch dough down. Shape half of dough into small balls. Place on greased baking sheets. Cover with plastic wrap and foil, sealing well. Freeze until firm. Transfer to plastic bags. Freeze up to four weeks.

For orange sugar buns: Shape remaining dough into small balls. Dip each into melted butter, then coat with prepared orange sugar (dry mixture of sugar and grated orange peel) and place, not touching, on baking sheet. Let rise in a warm place, free from drafts, until more than double in bulk (about 1½ hours). Bake in preheated 350° oven for 25 to 30 minutes or until done. Remove from pan and cool on wire rack.

Makes about 2 dozen rolls.

To bake frozen rolls: Remove from freezer; place on greased baking sheets. Cover; let rise in warm place, free from drafts, until doubled in bulk (about 1½ hours). Bake at 350° for 15 minutes, or until golden brown and done. Remove from baking sheets and cool on wire rack.

Makes about 2 dozen rolls.

To bake frozen rolls: Remove from freezer; place on greased baking sheets. Cover; let rise in warm place, free from drafts, until doubled in bulk (about 1½ hours). Bake at 350° for 15 minutes, or until golden brown and done. Remove from baking sheets and cool on wire rack.

Makes about 2 dozen rolls.

12

That Something Sweet

CAKE LAYERS

3½ cups all-purpose flour
2 tablespoons baking powder
½ teaspoon salt
½ pound butter, room temperature
2 cups sugar
1 cup milk
2 tablespoons brandy, kirsch or sherry

Grease and flour four 8-inch round layer cake pans. Sift flour with baking powder and salt. Cream butter with sugar, beat until sugar has dissolved. Mix dry ingredients alternately with liquid ingredients, blending well after each addition. Pour batter into prepared pans. Bake at 375° 25 to 30 minutes or until cakes test done. Let stand at room temperature for 10 minutes. Turn out onto cake racks, let stand until cool. Wrap layers separately and freeze.

QUICK-TO-THE-TABLE LAYER CAKE

Put together two cake layers with currant jelly between. Cover with whipped cream frosting. Store in refrigerator or freezer until ready to serve.

WHIPPED CREAM FROSTING

1 cup heavy cream
2 tablespoons confectioners' sugar
1 to 2 tablespoons brandy, kirsch, dry sherry, rum or any desired liqueur

Beat cream until stiff. Fold in remaining ingredients.

Variations

Sprinkle iced cake with shredded coconut, chopped walnuts, or slivered almonds or dribble melted bittersweet chocolate over top of cake.

CAKE and ICE CREAM PIE

You don't always have to ice cake layers. For a really delicious dessert, simply cut a cake layer into pie shape wedges, top with ice cream and ladle sauce over top. For instance: Top cake layer with butter pecan ice cream. Spoon rum sauce over top.

Rum Sauce

2 tablespoons butter
4 tablespoons confectioners' sugar
2 tablespoons light rum
1 cup heavy cream

Melt butter, stir in sugar and rum. Beat cream until stiff, fold in butter-sugar-rum mixture.

Or top cake wedge with strawberry ice cream. Ladle foamy sauce (below) over top.

Foamy Sauce

2 eggs
1 cup sugar

2 tablespoons brandy or kirsch
1 cup heavy cream

Put eggs and sugar in top half of double boiler over simmering water and beat with whisk until about triple in volume. Let cool to lukewarm. Add brandy or kirsch. Beat cream until stiff, fold in egg-sugar mixture. Store in refrigerator until ready to use.

Or top cake wedges with peach ice cream and ladle Melba sauce over top.

Melba Sauce

1 10-ounce package frozen raspberries
2 tablespoons kirsch

Break up frozen block of raspberries. Place in electric blender. Add kirsch and blend to a puree. Serve while still icy cold.

FROZEN PECAN COOKIES

1 cup white sugar
1 cup light brown sugar
½ cup (1 stick) butter
2 eggs, lightly beaten
¼ teaspoon salt
1 teaspoon vanilla
1 teaspoon baking soda
3 cups flour
1 cup chopped pecans

Cream white and brown sugar with butter. Add eggs and beat until well blended. Add vanilla and salt. Sift soda and flour together, gradually fold into egg, butter and sugar mixture. Fold in pecans. Turn out onto a lightly floured board and form into a long roll 1 to 2 inches thick. Cut roll into three parts. Place on cookie sheet or foil, freeze until firm, then wrap in foil and store in freezer.*

To serve: With a sharp knife, cut off as many cookies as desired. Bake in a 350° oven until crisp and brown (about 15 minutes).

Makes about 4 dozen.

CHEESE PIE GRAND MARNIER

Crust

1½ cups graham cracker crumbs.
 ¼ cup sugar
 ¼ teaspoon cinnamon
 ⅛ teaspoon nutmeg
 1 teaspoon grated orange rind
 ½ cup melted butter

Filling

 3 3-ounce packages cream cheese, softened
 ½ cup sugar
 3 eggs
 2 tablespoons Grand Marnier liqueur

*To serve without freezing, chill in refrigerator 4 to 6 hours before baking at 350° for 30 minutes.

Topping

1 cup sour cream
2 tablespoons brown sugar
2 tablespoons grated orange rind
2 tablespoons Grand Marnier

Combine graham cracker crumbs, sugar, cinnamon, nutmeg, orange rind and butter. Blend well. Press firmly into sides and bottom of a 9-inch buttered pie pan. Bake 8 minutes at 350°. Cool before filling. Combine cream cheese, sugar, eggs, and Grand Marnier. Blend to whipped cream consistency. Pour into cooled pie shell. Bake at 350° for 15 to 20 minutes or until firm. Cool in refrigerator or freezer. Combine sour cream, brown sugar, orange rind and Grand Marnier. Spread on cheese filling.* Freeze until firm. Then wrap and store in freezer.

To serve: Unwrap, let stand at room temperature for 5 to 10 minutes before cutting.

Serves 6 to 8.

BLACK DEVIL PIE

1 frozen pie shell (see recipe, p. 172)
1 pint chocolate ice cream
½ pint heavy cream
2 tablespoons sugar
3 tablespoons rum or cognac
1 2-ounce square of unsweetened chocolate

*To serve without freezing, bake for 30 to 40 minutes, sprinkle with cheese, and return to oven until cheese melts.

Place frozen pie shell in preheated 450° oven and bake for 10 to 15 minutes or until lightly browned. Remove shell from oven and place in freezer until thoroughly chilled. Remove ice cream from freezer and allow to soften slightly. Whip heavy cream with sugar until very stiff. Fill chilled pie shell with alternating scoops of whipped cream and ice cream, piling high in a mound. Dribble rum or cognac over pie and sprinkle with grated chocolate. Return to freezer until firm. Allow to stand for 5 to 10 minutes at room temperature before serving.*

Serves 6 to 8.

FROZEN PINEAPPLE CHEESE PIE

1 8-ounce package cream cheese
2 tablespoons milk
3 pints vanilla ice cream
  cream
½ pint pineapple sherbet
1 baked frozen vanilla crumb crust (see recipe, p. 172)
1 8-ounce can unsweetened crushed pineapple, well drained

Bring cream cheese to room temperature. Beat with milk in a large chilled bowl until very soft and creamy. Let ice cream and sherbet soften slightly, add to cream cheese and beat with electric mixer until blended. Press mixture firmly into crumb pie shell. Freeze until firm. Wrap and seal in foil.

To serve: Chill well-drained crushed pineapple in refrigerator. Unwrap frozen pie, spoon chilled pineapple over surface and press down firmly. Let stand at room temperature about 15 minutes before slicing.

Serves 6 to 8.

*If pie is to be made ahead, freeze until firm then wrap tightly in foil and seal.

BRANDIED ALASKA PIE
and
BLACK BOTTOM PIE

For the Crusts

¼ pound butter
3 cups graham cracker crumbs
1 cup confectioners' sugar

For the Black Bottom Pie

2 squares unsweetened chocolate
½ cup sugar
5 tablespoons water
2 tablespoons coffee liqueur (or brandy)
1 quart coffee ice cream
½ pint sour cream

For the Brandied Alaska Pie

1 quart butter pecan ice cream
¼ cup brandy
3 egg whites
¼ teaspoon cream of tartar
6 tablespoons sugar

To prepare crusts: Melt butter in a large skillet, stir in crumbs and sugar. Press mixture firmly into the bottoms and sides of two 9-inch pie tins. Bake in preheated 350° oven for 8 to 10 minutes. Cool. Freeze until firm.

For the black bottom pie: Place chocolate, sugar, water and coffee liqueur (or brandy) in container of electric blender and blend until smooth. Pour over bottom of one crumb pie shell. Freeze until firm. Press coffee ice cream over chocolate bottom and into side of shell. Pour coffee liqueur (or brandy) over surface. Cover with sour cream. Freeze until firm. Wrap and store in freezer. Serve frozen.

For the brandied Alaska pie: Fill frozen crumb shell with butter pecan ice cream. Pour brandy over surface. Return to freezer until very firm (about 2 hours). Beat egg white with cream of tartar until stiff. Fold in sugar, beat until glossy. Remove pie from freezer. Spread meringue over ice cream, sealing edges carefully to enclose ice cream. Place pie on a bread board or place in a shallow pan of crushed ice and bake at 450° until meringue is lightly browned (4 or 5 minutes). Serve at once or immediately return pie to freezer until time to serve. Serve within 1 or 2 hours

PINEAPPLE CHEESE CAKE (to enjoy now)
and
CHERRY BRANDY CHEESE CAKE (for the freezer)

Vanilla Crumb Crust

3 cups vanilla wafer crumbs
½ cup melted butter
2 tablespoons water

For the Basic Cheese Cake

4 8-ounce packages cream cheese, room temperature
6 egg yolks
1½ cups sugar
4 tablespoons flour
½ teaspoon salt
⅔ cup evaporated milk
6 egg whites

For the Pineapple Cheese Cake

1 8-ounce can crushed pineapple, thoroughly drained

For the Cherry Brandy Cheese Cake

2 tablespoons sweet maraschino cherry liqueur, kirsch,
   kümmel, or brandy
1 1-pound can pitted Bing cherries
½ cup sugar
2 tablespoons cornstarch
2 or 3 drops red food coloring

For the crust: Combine wafer crumbs, melted butter and water. Press over bottoms and sides of two 9-inch spring-form pans or any pan with a removable bottom. Bake at 350° for 5 minutes, remove from oven and cool.

For the basic cheese cake: Beat cream cheese until fluffy. Beat in egg yolks, sugar, flour and salt. When smooth beat in undiluted evaporated milk. Beat egg whites until stiff and fold into cheese mixture.

For pineapple cheese cake: Cover bottom of one crumb crust pan with crushed pineapple, pour half of cheese batter into pan. Bake at 350° for 1 hour or until firm. Cool and chill. Serve cold.

For cherry cheese cake: Fold liqueur into remaining batter, and pour into second crumb crust lined pan. Bake at 350° for 1 hour or until firm. Cool. Remove from pan. Freeze until firm. Wrap and freeze.

To serve: Let stand at room temperature while preparing topping. Drain cherries and set aside, saving liquid. Cook ½ cup cherry liquid, sugar and cornstarch over medium heat until reduced to a thick syrup. Stir in food coloring. Arrange cherries over top of cake. Pour syrup over surface. Refrigerate until ready to serve.

BAKED ALASKA JUBILEE

    1 9-inch cake layer (from the freezer)
    ¾ cup sugar
    1 to 1½ pints cherry or vanilla ice cream
    ¾ cup brandy
    7 tablespoons sugar plus ½ cup sugar
    1 1-pound can pitted Bing cherries
    1 tablespoons cornstarch
    4 egg whites
    ⅛ teaspoon cream of tartar

Place frozen cake layer in a shallow freezer-to-oven-to-table baking dish. Pour ¼ cup brandy over surface and sprinkle with 1 tablespoon of the sugar. Spread with a thick layer of ice cream, leaving a half inch "free" rim around cake. Place in freezer while preparing sauce and meringue. Combine cherries, cherry juice and 6 tablespoons sugar in a saucepan and bring to a boil. Lower heat and stir in cornstarch. Stir until thickened. Remove from heat and set aside.

Prepare meringue: Beat egg whites with cream of tartar until stiff. Fold in sugar. Beat until glossy. Completely cover cake and ice cream with meringue. Place in preheated 450° oven and bake until meringue is golden and flecked with brown. Warm remaining brandy in a small saucepan over moderate heat. Reheat cherries and sauce. Pour around cake. Ignite warmed brandy and pour flaming over cherries and sauce. Rush flaming to the table to serve as soon as flame subsides.

Serves 6 to 8.

ICE CREAM TARTS

Strawberry Tarts

Vanilla wafer crumb crust tart shells (see recipe, p. 172)
Strawberry ice cream
Fresh strawberries, sliced and sugared
Whipped cream

Press slightly softened strawberry ice cream into crumb crust with a spoon, leaving center indentation. Freeze until ready to serve. Fill center with fresh sliced, sugared strawberries and top with whipped cream.

Peach Tarts

Do the same with peach ice cream. Fill center with fresh peaches, sugared and sliced.

Coffee Tarts

Put coffee ice cream in walnut crumb shells (see page 173).
Serve with chocolate sauce. Sprinkle chopped walnuts over
and top with a dab of sour cream.

CRUMB CRUSTS

Chocolate Cookie Crumb Crust

 ¼ pound butter
35 thin chocolate wafers
 1 tablespoon confectioners' sugar

Melt butter over low heat in a large skillet. Remove from
heat, crush chocolate wafers into fine crumbs. Stir into butter,
add sugar and blend. Press firmly into six individual tart pans.
Bake at 300° for 10 minutes. Freeze until firm. Stack with
waxed paper or foil between each. Wrap, stacked in foil or seal
in plastic bag. Store in freezer until needed.

Brandy Graham Cracker Crust

 ¼ pound butter
1½ cups graham cracker crumbs
 ½ cup confectioners' sugar
 6 teaspoons brandy

Melt butter, stir in crumbs and sugar. Press into six tart pans. Sprinkle each with a teaspoon of brandy. Bake at 300° for ten minutes. Freeze until firm. Stack with waxed paper or foil between each tart shell. Wrap, stack in foil or plastic bag, freeze.

Walnut Crumb Crust

¼ pound butter
1½ cups vanilla wafer crumbs
¼ cup ground walnuts

Melt butter, stir in crumbs and walnuts. Press into six tart pans. Bake at 300° for 10 minutes. Freeze as above.

Index